Schelling's Dialogical *Freedom Essay*

SUNY Series in Contemporary Continental Philosophy

Dennis J. Schmidt, editor

SCHELLING'S DIALOGICAL *FREEDOM ESSAY*

Provocative Philosophy Then and Now

BERNARD FREYDBERG

STATE UNIVERSITY OF NEW YORK PRESS

Published by
STATE UNIVERSITY OF NEW YORK PRESS, ALBANY

Printed in the United States of America

For information, contact
State University of New York Press, Albany, NY
www.sunypress.edu

Production by Marilyn P. Semerad
Marketing by Michael Campochiaro

Library of Congress Cataloging-in-Publication Data

Freydberg, Bernard, 1947–
Schelling's dialogical freedom essay : provocative philosophy then and now / Bernard Freydberg.
p. cm. — (SUNY series in contemporary continental philosophy)
Includes bibliographical references and index.
ISBN 978-0-7914-7603-1 (hardcover : alk. paper)
ISBN 978-0-7914-7604-8 (paperback : alk. paper) 1. Schelling, Friedrich Wilhelm Joseph von, 1775–1854. Philosophische Untersuchungen über das Wesen der menschlichen Freiheit. 2. Liberty. 3. Good and evil. I. Title.

BJ1463.S356F74 2008
123'.5—dc22

2007052830

10 9 8 7 6 5 4 3 2 1

For Akiko
Eternally

Contents

Acknowledgments

A draft of *Schelling's Dialogical* Freedom Essay: *Provocative Philosophy Then and Now* was prepared during a 2005–2006 sabbatical at Slippery Rock University, Slippery Rock, PA, and received its final treatment during the summer of 2007, as I awaited the beginning of my work at Koç University in Istanbul, Turkey. Schelling's thought, from beginning to end, issues from and is shaped by *imagination.* In addition to the primary inspiration provided by Schelling's thought, I have had the exceptional good fortune of friendships and conversations with people of considerable imagination. By this, I certainly mean philosophers who work in Schelling, such as John Sallis, Dennis Schmidt, Jason Wirth, Richard Findler, Peter Warnek, and David Farrell Krell.

I certainly also include other philosophical colleagues (in alphabetical order): Sara Brill, Walter Brogan, Andrew Colvin, Katherine Cooklin, Daniel Dahlstrom, Gregory Recco, Francisco Gonzalez, Karen Gover, Elizabeth Hoppe, Drew Hyland, Robert Metcalf, Michael Naas, Gregory Recco, James Risser, David Roochnik, John Rose, Michael Rudar, John Russon, John and Jerry Sallis, Eric Sanday, Susan Schoenbaum, Charles Scott, Gary Scott, P. Christopher Smith, Sonja Tanner, and Bradley Wilson.

My new administrators and colleagues at Koç University in Istanbul have provided a welcoming and encouraging environment within which I prepared the final text. I wish to thank President Attíla Aşkar, Provost Yaman Arkun, Dean Ersin Yurtsever, and Associate Dean Sami Gülgöz. It is an honor to work for all of them. My two new philosophy colleagues, Patrick Roney and Hulya Durudoğan, have already taught me a great deal, and are both excellent teachers and delightful people. I also acknowledge our fine department assistant Deniz Durmuş, and our magnificent secretary Filiz Koca.

Two anonymous readers at SUNY Press provided encouraging comments and helpful suggestions, both of which clearly improved the book. It was a delight to work with Jane Bunker, Editor in Chief of SUNY Press, Director of Production Marilyn Semerad, Copyeditor Amy Paradysz, and Andrew Kenyon, assistant to Ms. Bunker.

The superb staff of Bailey Library always made sure I received all necessary materials promptly. Kathleen Manning, Rita McClelland and Christine Agostino have my abiding appreciation for this, and for being such agreeable people with whom to work.

Exponential good fortune in every direction comes my way from Akiko Kotani, my wife. She is a first-rate original contemporary artist, and a challenging, articulate speaker and writer about artistic matters. Our dinner table is the site of many spirited discussions, and to say that I learn much from them would understate the case considerably. The book cover shows her "T-Square," created in honor of the Chinese freedom-lover's courageous stand at Tieneman Square in 1989.

Michael Rudar, listed above among my philosophical colleagues, has once again done a wonderful job proofreading. When he finishes his graduate work at Duquesne University, he will be a most welcome addition in every way as a professor in the department fortunate enough to hire him.

My final acknowledgment goes to my daughter Malika, who exceeds my imagination in the pleasure and in the pride that I take in her.

Introduction

RECENT AND WELCOME interest in Schelling, especially as a result of the work of Jason Wirth, has provoked me to offer a reading of Schelling's 1809 *Freedom Essay*[1] that maps out three related but distinct paths. The first, with which I shall conclude this very brief introductory remark, concerns the relation of several of Schelling's philosophical issues to our own in Continental philosophy. Below, I will pose four specific questions here that address this relation. In the initial part of this book's two-part conclusion, I will answer them based upon this Schelling-interpretation.

The second, this book's longest and widest pathway, excavates the *Freedom Essay*'s sustained dialogue with what for Schelling is the always provocative philosophical history that preceded it. In this part, I attempt to demonstrate not only Schelling's exceptional feeling for the tradition (for this he has received both praise and blame), but also the surprisingly subtle scholarship that informs this feeling. This dialogue, in my view, provides a kind of model for philosophical dialogue in our own age. I will show, therefore, that its excavation and display has a result that could not be further from a mere archeological or historical curiosity.[2]

Thus, I hope to establish beyond question that Schelling's *Freedom Essay* holds vital importance for us, a view that is gradually but unmistakably emerging. This is so not because of a serendipitous timeliness but for the opposite reason: Many matters he treats are indeed crucial to the pursuit of wisdom but have been given short shrift both by Continental thinkers and by their Anglo-American counterparts. I propose the following thesis, that much of the new attention that Schelling's thought currently receives is due precisely to its *untimeliness*. By way of introduction I shall list four such matters. Continental philosophy has surely treated each of them. However, a thoughtful dialogue—along the lines of Schelling's own with Plato, Kant and significant others—will enable a more rewarding engagement.

1. System: For Schelling, the presence of both philosophy and the world as *systematic* is virtually assumed as given. Why? Why has system fared so poorly in recent and contemporary philosophy?
2. Logic: For Schelling, the logical copula expressed a living relation. Logic is thought most fundamentally in terms of the Greek *logos*. Why? How has the copula, and how has logic in general, come to be conceived and interpreted as formal?
3. Darkness: For Schelling, darkness resided at the heart of all disclosure as its living basis. The role of concealment in all disclosure has been, since Heidegger, widely acknowledged and considered. What might Schelling's *Freedom Essay* add to this consideration?
4. Divinity: For Schelling, divine experience is an ever-ongoing presence. In Anglo-American philosophy, such talk is an embarrassment. In Continental philosophy, God is present in an oblique fashion, if at all. Can Schelling's thought be brought into fruitful dialogue with either or both?

Finally, the third path should be marked "under construction." In it, I provide my own meditation on philosophy today and upon the necessary presence of Schelling for such a meditation. I will speak of Heidegger and of Derrida, but the dialogical "pavement" will be that provided by John Sallis. His chapters on Schelling in *Delimitations* and in *Chorology* provide remarkable philosophical insight in themselves. However, since they are the concluding chapters of both books, and since Schelling is virtually never the last thinker taken up in a major work of contemporary Continental philosophy, these chapters are pathbreaking and courageous as well.

As to the originality of Schelling's thought, Schelling himself distinguishes work that is genuinely original (*ursprünglich*) from work that is merely novel (*original*). Genuine originality in philosophy springs from creative appropriation of the history of philosophy. Many thinkers play a role in the *Freedom Essay*, and they will be studied in the context of the essay: Heraclitus (by implication), Sextus Empiricus, Spinoza, Leibniz, and others. However, the two whose thought essentially shaped the *Freedom Essay* are Plato, among the ancients, and Kant, among the moderns. In a footnote on 409, Schelling writes that the matters in the essay arise in the manner of a conversation (*gesprächsweise*), and he claims that he could have made things clearer had he not done so. This conversation points in two directions. First, it points to the reader, who is enjoined to put forth the effort to think with the author, to question and respond to the *logos* of the *Freedom Essay*. At the same time, it points to Plato and Kant, his two principal interlocutors. I shall argue that the *Freedom Essay* is a creative synthesis of Kant and Plato at its heart, reducible to neither, and as such it clears a new pathway toward Nietzsche and into the Continental philosophy of the twentieth and twenty-first centuries.

Schelling's Dialogical Freedom Essay: *Provocative Philosophy Then and Now* is itself intended conversationally, though my interpretation takes the shape of a textual exegesis. Paradigms of the exegesis are Heidegger's *Kant and the Problem of Metaphysics* and *Schelling's Treatise on the Essence of Human Freedom*. In line with the adage that no good deed goes unpunished, I take issue with Heidegger's magnificent Schelling-interpretation from which I learned so much. I depart from these only by addition: Discussions of Schelling literature are available in the Notes.

I maintain that the connections—syntheses of arguments and imaginative leaps—in Schelling's *Freedom Essay* are established first and foremost by inspired living recollections of the history of philosophy that reside not only consciously in his intellect but also viscerally in his bones and nervous system. An intriguing account of this procedure occurs in an article by Martin Wallen, with the rather unusual title "The Electromagnetic Orgasm and the Narrative of Primordiality," an interpretation of Schelling's *The Ages of the World*. Wallen notes, quite astutely in my view, that Schelling contains what he calls "an electromagnetic history" that reveals itself in "the dialogue form."[3] Unlike *Bruno, or on the Natural and Divine Principle of Things*, neither the *Freedom Essay* nor (for that matter) *The Ages of the World* comes complete with exchanges between interlocutors. "The dialogue form" refers rather to the inner dialogue of the thinker with the often fragmentary ebb and flow of the internalized visceral history, and to the full participation of the reader who is as much provided with a map for a journey as is given a series of philosophical claims. I will employ the tools of the scholar as both an entry to this participation and as a "travel guide" to many of the noteworthy locations on this map.

Readers of Schelling therefore must arrive as thinkers in our own right, ready for a journey upon which each of us embarks. I hope, therefore, that *Schelling's Dialogical* Freedom Essay: *Provocative Philosophy Then and Now* succeeds in articulating key aspects of that dialogue and key signposts to aid on that journey. The goal is not doctrinal. Indeed, the absence of such a goal is both the enticement and the challenge of Schelling's thought. Rather, the goal is to retrieve—for this author as well as for kindred spirits—the once-vital capacity for rapture-infused rigor that characterized the thought of this philosopher called by Heidegger "the most genuinely creative and by far the farthest reaching (*ausgreifende*) thinker in this entire era of German philosophy."[4]

NOTE ON THE TEXTS

All Schelling texts have been taken from the Manfred Schröter edition of Schelling's works (*Schellings Werke*, Münchener Jubilaumausdruckes, 1959). Footnotes refer to the Schröter volume numbers, original volume numbers and original page numbers respectively (i.e., in the German style). Although I have, upon occasion, consulted available translations of Schelling's work that are listed in the bibliography, all translations are mine.

Since the available translations of Kant are far more reliable than those of Schelling, I have, for the most part, adhered to them, although I did change wording occasionally. The texts of Plato have been taken from the Oxford Edition (*Platonic Opera*, ed. Ioannes Burnet, Oxford, 1967), to which all footnotes refer. Translations are mine, although again I have consulted available ones, which are listed in the bibliography.

I

The Unfolding of the Task

THE FIRST TWO sentences of the work read:

> Philosophical investigations concerning the essence of human freedom can in part concern the right concept of freedom, for although the feeling of freedom is immediately stamped in each, the fact of freedom lies in no way so near to the surface that merely to express it in words would not require a more than usual purity and depth of sense; in part the investigations can concern the connection (*Zusammenhang*) of this concept with the whole of a scientific (*wissenschaftlichen*) world-view. Since however, no concept can be determined separately, and the demonstration of its connection with the whole also first provides the final scientific completion, this must especially be the case with the concept of freedom since, if it is to have reality in general (*überhaupt Realität*), it must be no mere subordinate or incidental concept, but rather one of the governing central points (*Mittelpunkte*) of the system: therefore, both these sides of the investigation here fall together into one (*fallen . . . in eins zusammen*).[1] (336)

Like the long, dense opening sentence of Kant's *Critique of Practical Reason*, Schelling's first words invite and require much unpacking. In them, the entire problematic of the *Freedom Essay* is traced out. These first words contain neither declarations nor theses, and they are as far as possible from being arbitrary assertions. Rather, they are *provocations*. As philosophical provocations, they are not just external spurs to thought. Rather, provocation itself belongs to the nature of Schelling's thought. As I will attempt to show in what follows, such provocations drive the movement of this text from a necessarily unresolved matter to its subsequent plane. The essay even concludes with a further provocation.

In service to the task of unpacking Schelling's introductory words, I offer the following:

1. Philosophical investigations, properly understood, do not occur in parts, the sum of which comprises a whole. Rather, the whole provides and pervades parts. Together with fellow students Fichte, Hegel, and Hölderlin, Schelling shared a passion for Spinoza and the ambition to fashion a unified system of philosophy. Their motto was "*hen kai pan*," "the one and the all," which recalls the "*hen panta*" ("one is all") of Heraclitus.[2] For Schelling, one and all, part and whole, are the same. The demonstration of the connection of parts with the whole *first* provides the final (*letzte*) completion. Thus, whereas philosophical investigations are presented in parts and successively, in the ultimate sense part and whole are simultaneous. One can speak of the sameness of first and last. But how? This is the first provocation that will lead into the *Freedom Essay* proper.

It is worth noting that Schelling begins the first sentence by speaking in the plural ("investigations") and concludes the second by speaking of sides of a (singular) investigation. This suggests that the task of philosophical investigation itself involves gathering a many into a one, gathering parts into the whole, serving as the place where they show their sameness. Another provocation: How can mere investigation accomplish such a task?

2. Philosophical investigations are by their nature bound up with *science* and *system*. "*Science* in general—its content may be whatever it will—is a whole that stands under the form of unity. This is only possible insofar as all parts of it are subordinated to *one* condition; each part, however, is determined by another only insofar as it itself is determined through that one condition."[3] System comes from the Greek *sunhistamai* meaning "to stand together" (*sun-* "together"; *histemi*, "stand"). In Greek, the word we normally translate as science, *episteme*, also includes *histemi*. In attending to the Greek, one can discern the kinship of science and system for Schelling more easily.

The German, *Wissenschaft*, might best be rendered in English as "'state' of knowing" (*Wissen-schaft*). One would therefore miss the core of Schelling's thought by reading in our contemporary understanding of science, either as a nominal heading for the natural (and/or human) sciences or as a particular disciplinary method of inquiry. Philosophy as system of science means that philosophy articulates the unity of the whole as such. The system of science is the presentation of *hen kai pan*.[4]

3. Philosophical investigations require an unusual purity and depth. "The realm of the sciences is not a democracy, still less an ochlocracy, but an aristocracy in the most precious sense."[5] For Schelling, philosophy is esoteric by nature. While this most certainly implies the division of the many and the excellent few, *hoi polloi* and *hoi aristoi*, nothing may be concluded concerning the *personal* superiority or authority of the philosopher. The philosopher is philosopher by virtue of being gathered into philosophy, "called" by philosophy. One cannot reverse this and say that philosophy is what philosophers choose or produce. Philosophy itself is the measure, dividing the few from the many.

The name of that unusual insight that the philosopher has been granted is *intellectual intuition*: "the point . . . in which the o b j e c t (O *b j e k t*) and its concept, the o b j e c t (G *e g e n s t a n d*)[6] and its representation are originally, absolutely and without all mediation one."[7] Although Kant insisted that for human beings intuition must be sensuous and not intellectual, his followers Fichte and Schelling both placed intellectual intuition at the heart of their systems. The following might serve as way of access to this notion: Think as if the duality between the sensible and the intelligible elements of our knowing were suddenly to disappear, such that we behold the source of their unity in an instant. Schelling remarks: "Why by this intuition something mysterious (*etwas Mysteriöses*)—a special sense only amidst several—there is no ground except that in many this sense is actually lacking, which however is without doubt no stranger than the fact than other senses are lacking in many others, the reality of which can just as little be brought into doubt."[8]

In other words, an artistic sense may be present in few but lacking in many. The same can be said of a mathematical sense, or even an athletic one. Thus the lack of intellectual intuition is no reproach of any kind, any more than its presence redounds to the credit of its possessor. These various "senses" are meted out, and should be seen as partial articulations of the whole, of the system of science. Nevertheless, the aforementioned citation implies that the realm of the sciences is ordered hierarchically.

Something of this hierarchy presents itself already in the first sentence, where Schelling points to a split within the showing of freedom. Freedom is *given* in feeling, and *given to each, immediately*. Thus, there is no hierarchy with respect to the feeling of freedom. However, the fact (*Tatsache*) of freedom is distinguished from the feeling. The feeling announces the fact, but gives nothing determinate regarding the fact. The feeling is given on the surface, immediately available to all. The fact lies deeper. Thus, in the feeling of freedom, the fact of freedom is at once made manifest and concealed. To say this another way, in feeling freedom is brought to light as dark. Its presence is given immediately, but its essence, *what* it is, lies concealed.

Thus an investigation, a deed, an *undertaking* is necessary in order to bring the essence of human freedom to the fore. The task is to bring freedom to words, so that what freedom is becomes manifest in speech, in *logos*. In other words, the task is to articulate the inarticulate feeling and so unite the *that* of freedom with its *what*. This is why philosophical investigations into the essence of human freedom concern the right concept: The right concept is the one in which freedom is brought out of the realm of feeling, and into the realm of *logos*. For such investigations, the special philosophical sense is required.

Several issues present themselves: What is the relation of the threefold of feeling, fact, and concept?[9] Does the feeling serve as a mere clue to the concept, or perhaps does the movement from feeling to concept occur for the sake of the fact? Also, in what sense, if at all, is the bringing to articulation of the inarticulate feeling of freedom itself an act of freedom? Or in other words, insofar as philosophy involves articulation, involves bringing matters to *logos*, in what way is *philosophy* involved with freedom? And, since the expression of the fact of freedom in words is not immediate as the feeling is but requires mediation, how does the character of the mediation belong together with the movement from mute feeling to articulate concept? Further, if the bringing to *logos* of freedom is the task of philosophical investigations, through what will this "bringing" occur?

Some indication of the direction toward which one might look in order to grasp these issues can be found in the other "part" of philosophical investigations mentioned in the first sentence, together with the second sentence. The concept of freedom must be connected with the whole of a scientific worldview, but for this concept to have "reality in general" it must be "one of the central points" of the system. Looking aside for a moment from the provocation of suggesting that a unified system has more than one central point, why must the concept of freedom belong to the center of the system? Reality, with its Latin root *res*, roughly means "thinghood," what belongs to an actual thing. The essence of freedom requires its absolute presence in and throughout the system (i.e., *überhaupt*), because if at any point it was absent (that is, thwarted in its being), this would contradict its very nature: Freedom would not be freedom, which is impossible.

Returning to the aforementioned provocation of plural centers, this provides a glimpse of the struggle that will be required to attain the right concept of freedom, and so to complete the whole of the scientific world-view. In other Schellingian language, the articulation of freedom is bound up with the articulation of system. And since the two are not parts in the sense of distinct, heterogeneous elements of an aggregate whole, but are rather both ultimately the same, the articulation of freedom is *nothing but* the articulation of system. And as system is as far as possible from being an ordering frame externally imposed upon material that is somehow separate from it, for Schelling the articulation of freedom is at once the articulation of the world.

To articulate freedom, that is, to bring freedom to *logos*, requires mediation. But in light of the intellectual intuition of the philosopher, it is not at all clear why such mediation is required. Given the immediate connection of concept and object, why can't the essence of freedom simply be asserted, in the manner of much more mundane analytic propositions in which the predicate is contained immediately in its subject? The key to this riddle is that these investigations have in view *human* freedom. In human freedom, the clue to the articulation of the world is present, since it is freedom and since the articulation of freedom is one with the articulation of the world. Since it is human and therefore given over to finitude, this freedom stands at a distance from the *complete* articulation of the world.

The *assertion* that freedom must be one of the dominant central points arises from intellectual intuition. However, "We cannot properly prove the essential identity of the real with the ideal even in philosophy. . . . All that can be proven is that without it there can be no science, and in everything that is a claim to knowledge, this identity or this entire process of the real into the ideal (and of the possibility of the full translation of the ideal into the real) is sighted."[10] With respect to freedom, this means that what is *thought* in its very concept implies its central position in the world. However, more than this implication is required, since the connection, because it is antecedent to all proof, cannot itself be proven. This *more*, this mediation that is needed to bring freedom and the world to *logos*, is the work (*ergon*) of philosophy.

Thus the world is to be disclosed in human freedom, and freedom is to be disclosed in the world—through the human being. The human being is therefore at once subject and object, and is such by virtue of freedom. It might therefore be said that the feeling of the fact of freedom shows man to himself as the sign of the world, a sign that requires an interpretation.

To say that the human being is at once sign and interpreter of sign provokes the question of the relation of the human being to himself. A way of access to this question that silently animates the entire *Freedom Essay*, as well as a beginning of the presentation of its inner appropriation of Kantian and Platonic philosophy, will be provided at this point.

Kant's first critique, the *Critique of Pure Reason*, limits knowledge, including self-knowledge, to appearances. The endeavor of the human being to know itself in its singular essence meets with frustration. It may seem that the transition of the thinking "I" of transcendental apperception through the categories to the thought-about "I" would make self-knowledge not only possible but also robust. We would know ourselves as substance (permanent), as simple (indissoluble), as personal (self-identical), and as immediately given to ourselves. Accordingly, we would have epistemological assurance of our real and meaningful immortality.

However, all these conclusions rest upon a transcendental illusion, which Kant calls "the subreption of the hypostasized consciousness":

> We can thus say of the thinking 'I' (the soul) . . . that it does *not* know *itself through the categories*, but knows the categories, and through them all objects, in the absolute unity of apperception, and so through itself. Now it is, indeed, very evident that I cannot know as an object that which I must presuppose in order to know any object, and that the determining self (the thought) is distinguished from the self that is to be determined (the thinking subject) as knowledge is to be distinguished from its object.[11]

Pure reason itself judges that human reason is incapable of providing us with the means to know ourselves in our essence. We can know ourselves only as given to ourselves from a distance, that is, through inner sense ruled by the categories. Self-ignorance belongs, then, to the essence of humanity. To say the very same thing from another perspective, something crucial is indeed known about humanity, namely that a certain measure of irremediable ignorance belongs to our essence. In the Paralogisms of Pure Reason, Kant reaches this conclusion regarding rational psychology, the metaphysical doctrine of the soul now humbled by the critique:

> But though it furnishes no positive doctrine, it reminds us that we should regard this refusal of reason to give satisfying response to our inquisitive probings into what is beyond the limits of this present life as reason's hint to divert our self-knowledge from fruitless and extravagant speculation to fruitful practical employment.[12]

Thus, although abysmally removed from ourselves with respect to knowledge, we are given back to ourselves with respect to *action*, in the moral realm. By means of free obedience to a law which human reason gives each human being, we have the means to live in a dignified manner befitting our finite nature. The moral law provides no theoretical knowledge. But its status as a necessary presupposition for morality allows it to serve both our possibilities and our limits. Regarding our possibilities, it offers us access to a realm beyond appearances. Regarding our limits, it acknowledges our finite nature both as self-ignorant and as subject to pathological needs. Both of these aspects are captured in one of Kant's most provocative observations, made in the *Foundations of the Metaphysics of Morals*: "It is in fact completely impossible by experience to discern with complete certainty a single case in which the maxim of an action . . . rested solely on moral ground . . ." (IV, 407). For Kant, the law-governed moral disposition, in its striving to determine human action, is the proper celebration of our rational nature, and this striving to bring our disposition into harmony with the demands of the moral life constitutes the appropriate relation of humanity itself.

Much of this echoes Socratic ignorance. A deep inner kinship exists between Kant and Plato regarding the necessary limit attaching to human knowledge. However, within this kinship an epochal distance asserts itself that will play a major role in Schelling's creative synthesis. In the *Apology*, Socrates speaks to the citizens of Athens of the oracle at Delphi that riddled that Socrates was the wisest of men. "Whatever does the god say, and whatever does he riddle about? I know that I am not wise, neither in great things nor in small things" (21b3–5). In service to the god Socrates sought to puzzle out the riddle, only to find all those whom he questioned in still more ignorant straits, possessing no more wisdom than that of the admitted ignorance of Socrates, but professing wisdom of the most glorious kind. Socrates concludes: "Oh men, I venture to say that the god is wise in reality, and that in this oracle, he says this—that human wisdom is worthy of something paltry and nothing at all. And it appears to me that in saying this, he means Socrates . . ." (23a5–7). The bridge from Socrates' ignorance to his wisdom is the god who has provided a "certain divine guide (*theion ti kai daimonion*)" (31c5–d1), which restrains him from crossing when such crossing is not well-fated, but which does not motivate action.

Thus followed Socrates' tale to his fellow Athenian citizens concerning the source of his activity. I am tempted to use a broad brush and to paint the Socratic *logos*, including the reference to his service to Apollo and his appeal to the *daimonion*, as an account in myth of what Kant, some two thousand years later, would demonstrate rationally. Despite having a measure of justification, such a conclusion fails to hear what peculiarly belongs to each account, and assumes that the matter is something independent of its expression. That is, it incorporates an underlying assumption, entirely unjustified, that language, *logos*, is a means. This assumption must be set aside if the *Freedom Essay* is to speak. Rather language, *logos*, is primarily speech as *showing, presentation* (*Darstellung*). It is important to note that in his tale, Socrates *sees himself mythically*. Immediately after saying that he did not think the god thought him wise, Socrates speaks in the voice of the god!

> . . . using my name, making me into a paradigm, as though he would say to men, "He among you is the wisest who, like Socrates, knows that his wisdom is really worth nothing at all." (23b2–4)

This self-inclusion in the myth goes beyond rhetoric. Socrates, as paradigm, is the one who understands himself mythically. The dialogue offers Socrates as a paradigm. But Socrates declares his own very peculiar paradigmatic statue *within a myth*. Socrates' activity in Athens is *logos*. The citation above, then, serves as a *muthos* of *logos*: as *mythology*. The paradigm of the relation of a human being to himself is not prescribed by law but shown in an image. Insofar as the image of Socrates attracts and delights human beings, inviting their vicarious participation, it can be called a *beautiful* image of humanity.

One of the earliest and most revealing of German Idealism writings insists upon the combination of rationality and mythology. Its title is "The Oldest System-Program of German Idealism," and its authorship is a matter of controversy. Different scholars have attributed it variously to Schelling, Hölderlin, and Hegel. Apart from the scholarly question, however, one can consider the document as a clue to and expression of one of the underlying impulses of the era. That Schelling could well have written it is supported by the subsequent quotations, as well as by his work as a whole:

> Until we have made the Ideas aesthetic, i.e., mythological, they are of no interest to the people; and conversely, until mythology has been made rational the philosopher can only be ashamed of it.[13]

The "Platonic Idea of Beauty" is to serve as the ultimate, with the highest act of reason "an aesthetic act."[14] According to this document, the task of philosophy is nothing other than the unification of reason and mythology, or in other words, the articulated exhibition of this unity. In his *Philosophy of Art—General Part* (1802), a work written in the manner of Spinoza's *Ethics*, Schelling explicitly works out the relation of mythology to the whole of philosophy. Socrates as a *beautiful* image of humanity? This peculiar claim can be better understood in light of Proposition Twenty, which reads: "Beauty and Truth are in themselves, or according to their idea, one."[15] In a crucial passage contained in an apparently minor note, Schelling explains, "Truth and beauty, just as goodness and beauty, never relate to one another as purpose and mean. . . ."[16] Therefore, beauty is no mere device by which the truth is presented in an enticing form. Rather, beauty is truth made intuitable. Truth is beauty made rational. The Socratic myth and the Kantian critiques occur successively, millennia apart. Schelling's *logos*, his "Proposition Twenty," gathers them into a simultaneous unity.

These remarks provide entry into Proposition Thirty-eight: "Mythology is the necessary condition and the first material of all art," the proposition to which "everything previous serves as proof. The *nervus probandi* lies in the idea of art as presentation of the absolute, of the beautiful in itself through particular beautiful things. . . ."[17] Therefore, mythology belongs essentially to the whole, the absolute. Through beauty, we apprehend the absolute. Through truth, we think it. The division of the two is merely apparent and ultimately illusory. It is a division that modern philosophy, conceived by Schelling as the presentation of the system of the whole, must overcome. In his *System of Transcendental Idealism*, Schelling writes, "What the intellectual intuition is for the philosopher, the aesthetical is for his object."[18] The two intuitions are essentially one. However, the modern interpretation of *logos* as reason, exemplified by Kant, seems to exclude mythology from the activity proper to a rational being. Rather, Kant's moral thought seems to require a radical split from everything that would motivate desire. The demand of reason for systematic completeness of its science seems far removed from the fashioning of images. Certainly, beauty plays a major role in Kant's third critique, the *Critique of Judgment*. This role, however, provides much provocation.

I will list and give brief comments on some of its major features: (1) the *Critique of Judgment* has the feeling of pleasure and pain as its realm. (The cognitive faculties constitute the realm of the *Critique of Pure Reason*; the faculties of desire constitute the realm of the *Critique of Practical Reason*.) (2) Beauty harmonizes reason and imagination without any concept, and so gives disinterested pleasure that is available in principle to all.

(3) However, the aesthetic judgment is a reflective and not a determinant judgment. It claims nothing about any object, but merely concerns the subject's self-relation. (4) Accordingly, beauty is quite separate from either the determinant judgments of science or the determinant judgments of morality. Kant calls the relation of reflective judgments to determinant judgments *symbolical.* Unlike the determinative relation of concepts, which he calls schematical, the symbolical relation is only indirect and analogical.[19] Therefore, beauty and truth, also beauty and goodness (morality), exist on entirely different planes for Kant. Accordingly, so too do reason and mythology.

These observations bear directly on the essence of humanity as determined thus far. Our relation to ourselves with respect to knowledge, that is, our knowing ignorance, sets the task of seeing ourselves as we are and of determining ourselves appropriately, and of accomplishing both in the face of this ignorance. In this way, Schelling's philosophical deed of bringing reason and mythology together arises from the divided condition of humanity as revealed thus far. It stems from the ignorance to which we are given over. It attempts to remedy this lack that separates us from ourselves by presenting the ultimate unity of the rational and the aesthetic that Kant at least seemed to deny.

The human being is a sign, but a sign of what? Schelling's unification of truth and beauty reinterprets the Kantian critiques and Socratic activity, in order to refresh the basic puzzle that was first sounded in the Delphic oracle.

❧

The first matter addressed threatens the entire enterprise. Freedom and system are held to be inconsistent (*unverträglich*). The unity and totality that are bound up with the concept of system exclude freedom by their very nature. This alleged inconsistency provides the provocation for the introduction and for the first of the investigations.

On the most fundamental level, the apparent clash of freedom and necessity is not a logical problem, nor is this clash something that can be treated from a distance. The clash is by its very nature provocative, calling forth a response that itself belongs to the meeting of freedom and necessity. "*Ti legei?*" is the Socratic question. What about this apparent inconsistency? An account, a *logos*, must be provided. The apparent clash of freedom and necessity therefore calls forth *philosophy*. Clearly, philosophy is not merely a doctrinal academic discipline for Schelling. Rather, philosophy issues from an existential anomaly that is fundamental to being human: (1) the co-presence in the human being of necessary laws of nature (of the systematic whole) to which the human being is bound and on which the human being depends, and (2) of freedom that signals a liberation and independence from these same necessary laws. Thus another way of saying that the human being is both sign and interpreter of sign is the following: The human being is both the question and the questioner.

Schelling notes that those who hold that freedom and system are inconsistent with one another might do so for any number of arbitrary reasons; he asserts that if indeed the two are mutually repugnant ". . . it is strange (*sonderbar*) that, since individual freedom is in some way connected with the world-whole . . . some system must be present, at least in the divine understanding, with which freedom coexists" (336–37). His explanation of this remark prefigures the intertwining that will manifest itself throughout the discourse, namely the essential togetherness of myth, science, and life:

> But whoever takes the theory of physics as his point of departure and knows that the doctrine "like is recognized by like" (supposed to come from Pythagoras but found in Plato and still earlier in Empedocles) is wholly ancient, will understand that the philosopher maintains such (divine) knowledge because he alone, keeping the understanding pure and undarkened by evil, conceives the god outside him with the god within him.[20] But those unfriendly toward science . . . understand by this knowledge something entirely abstract and lifeless. . . . (337)

The knowledge that would establish the coexistence of freedom and system falls alone to the philosopher, in whom science and life are gathered in a special way. The unfolding of the relation of freedom and system in the divine understanding makes itself manifest in the unfolding of philosophical knowledge. However, this provocation also calls for a response. How can the finitude of the philosopher, even gifted with intellectual intuition, attain the relation of freedom and system in the divine understanding? Since the presence of the divine guide is something given, unaccountable (as with Socrates, who proclaimed a "*theion ti kai daimonion*" [divine daimonic sign] but who claimed its rarity and/or uniqueness at *Republic* 496c2–4), the account of the philosopher must be mythological, must be a "likely account." Taking Schelling's thought beyond the context of these remarks, it suggests that in mythology, science and life receive their most appropriate expression. Though it may seem strange to root science in mythology, such great scientists as Heisenberg have done so in their own way.[21] Even the contemporary philosophy of science has lowered its voice to a whisper on the ultimate rationality of science.[22] Closer to the matter here, the togetherness of freedom and system must be told in a tale.

In no way, as Schelling will show, does putting freedom and system together imply logical incompatibility. Rather, even if they were logically compatible (which they are: see Kant's third antinomy and its modest solution),[23] this compatibility is insufficient to establish their togetherness. Schelling distinguishes philosophy from abstract and lifeless science, a class to which formal logic belongs. He specifically presents conventional geometry as his example. While the geometry of Euclid certainly can claim its measure of truth for the domain in which it holds away, that is, ideal objects in three-dimensional space in accord with its axioms and postulates, its objects are separated off from actual objects. The same, of course, is the case with logic. Modus ponens is surely valid, but its abstraction from actual objects means that infinitely many valid arguments can be constructed that do not correspond to anything encountered in the world. Geometry has long and often been regarded as exemplary for thinking, although it stops short of the highest thought for both Plato and Kant.[24]

For Schelling, geometry is insufficient and weak for one who would philosophize, not because it is wrong or even because it is limited, but because it is cut off from life. Freedom and system, then, must show themselves as occurring in and through life. They are expressed in a science that is a *living* science. Gradually, life will move to the center of the *Freedom Essay*. Schelling writes ". . . always, however, reason pressing towards unity as well as the feeling consisting of freedom and personality is denied only by decree . . . which finally must perish" (337). By implication, the yoked living forces of reason and feeling overcome the obstacles that have been placed in their way by prior developments in the history of thought that turned philosophy away from engagement with life.

At the end of the first paragraph, the relation of philosophy and life is more vividly presented. Not only must freedom and system show themselves in life; the clash of freedom and system *calls forth* life: "For this great task alone is the unconscious and invisible mainspring of all striving after knowledge, from the lowest to the highest; without the contradiction (*Widerspruch*) of freedom and necessity not only philosophy, but every higher willing of the spirit would sink to the death which is peculiar to those sciences in which this contradiction has no application" (338). Here, necessity (the necessity of the whole) and freedom are called *contradictory*.

However, the contradiction is necessary for living science, and serves as the concealed inspiration without which life could not first come forth.[25]

With an expression of the need to undergo this "business," the first paragraph of the *Freedom Essay* draws to a close. One might see in this most dense and condensed introduction not only preliminary remarks but also a presentation of the problematic of the *Freedom Essay*. Yet these matters, including that of the centrality of the contradiction of freedom and necessity, are given at some distance. They *announce* rather than enact what will come, in a matter befitting an introduction. In chapters II, III, and IV, Schelling will tacitly unfold the problematic as it flows from the unity of the threefold of feeling, fact, and concept, just as he expressly unfolds the necessary *agon* of freedom and necessity here. In chapter V, the results will be gathered up explicitly with regard to the aforementioned threefold, after which the interpretation will take up the deeper investigation into the essence of human freedom. This will also involve further "clarification" of that which resists being brought to clarity, namely the contradiction of freedom and necessity.

Since the contradiction of freedom and necessity serves as the goad for the *Freedom Essay*, surveying the contradiction from a distance is impossible by its very nature. In this regard, the conclusion of the first paragraph gains significance. One cannot opt for either freedom or necessity, although, if they are contradictory, one seemingly *must* opt for one or the other. Yet, "to withdraw from the conflict by foreswearing reason looks more like flight than victory. Another would have the same right to turn his back on freedom . . . without there being any cause for self-congratulations on either side" (338). Thus, the philosopher must *undergo* the contradiction of freedom and necessity, in order to arrive at the unwavering "concept of freedom, without which philosophy would be completely without value" (338). Schelling calls this a "necessary task." One can therefore say that in the task of philosophy freedom and necessity are bound, and that only by undergoing the deed, by doing the work of philosophy, by foreswearing flight, can one conceive freedom: *p a t h e i m a t h o s*.[26] ("Learn by suffering/undergoing.")

Freedom, Pantheism, and Idealism

THE NEXT TOPIC Schelling addresses is pantheism. One might wonder why this is the case. There had been a "pantheism controversy" (*Pantheismusstreit*) brought about by Lessing's endorsement of Spinozism in Germany, but it had ended by the late 1780s. Further, Kant found little to commend in Spinoza's thought. However, this historical accident did not discourage Schelling, who nevertheless saw pantheism as the only completed system of pure reason. It also serves to stand in for Kantian natural necessity, since Spinozism held that all things, including the human will, proceeded necessarily from the (rational) divine essence, which was identical with nature. Schelling's discussion of pantheism in its various manifestations is designed to show that pantheism, which he regards as a model system of reason, does not exclude freedom, and he provides a convincing demonstration of their copresence. In a deeper sense, however, the pantheism question raises the matters treated in the previous chapter into sharper relief. Early in the discussion, Schelling notes the place of the philosopher in the development of pantheism: "That the fatalistic sense can be combined with pantheism is undeniable; that it may not be essentially tied may be seen from the circumstance that so many have been driven to this point of view through the liveliest feeling of freedom" (339). The "liveliest feeling of freedom" serves as the clue to the solution of the pantheism question. Since the system of pantheism emerges from those with the liveliest sense of freedom, pantheism must itself be recognized as a product of freedom.

Schelling's task is to show pantheism as belonging to the essence of human freedom. The provocation is the following: Pantheism expresses the togetherness of reason's striving for wholeness, on the one hand, and the feeling of freedom, on the other. However, freedom is concealed *in* this expression. In this light, one can see the importance of pantheism in the *Freedom Essay*. Since the task is to bring freedom to *logos* and so to bring the feeling of freedom to the light of the right concept, pantheism—for which the feeling of freedom is its hidden origin and in which a scientific worldview is made manifest—must be encountered. Pantheism might therefore be regarded as the philosophical presentation of system, but as lacking the requisite wholeness because freedom is not to be found in its articulation.

Spinoza's *Ethics* presents pantheism in its exemplary form. However, *eros* is lacking in it. The absence of *eros* leaves the system of reason bereft of life and therefore abstract. Still more significantly, the absence of *eros* dooms the system to incompleteness even in a formal sense:

> How general the expressions are, that finite beings are modifications and consequences of God; what a cleft there is to be filled, what questions are to be answered! One could regard Spinozism in its rigidity like the statues of Pygmalion,[1] which had to be given a soul by the warm breath of love; but this comparison is incomplete since it more closely resembles a work projected only in the most external outlines, in which one would still notice the many lacking or incomplete features. It could more readily be compared to the oldest images of the godheads that, the fewer individually living features issuing from them, the more secret-bearing (*geheimnisvoller*) they appeared. (349–50)

The twofold of life and love are demanded not only for the presentation of the system of philosophy but for the completeness required by its concept. However, pantheism is neither wrong nor misguided, nor can it be ignored. The role of pantheism in the development of philosophy consists precisely in its *calling forth* of *eros*. This explains Schelling's judgment of the seductive secrecy of Spinozism. The need to encounter Spinozism can be seen as an erotic necessity, for in Spinozism one can discern an outline of that for which the philosopher strives. The philosopher can detect the likeness of the divine knowledge he discerns in Spinozism, and thus can enter into dialogue with it. For in Spinozism the *hen panta* makes itself dimly manifest, and *eros* the primordial unifier draws the philosopher's thought toward this veiled manifestation.

This deed-provoking attraction has several consequences. It accounts for the possibility of Spinozism as springing from a vision of unity. It accounts for the engagement with Spinozism, insofar as its form proves irresistible. Finally, it accounts for the overcoming of Spinozism, at least as a finished system, since the engagement exposes the life that was heretofore concealed in it. The principle of physics, "like to like" is itself a manifestation of *eros*. Thus, nature itself can only be understood with reference to erotic laws. The matter of the privation of *eros* in Spinozism is no mere side issue in Schelling's discussion. Rather, the absence of *eros* provides the depth and the unifying force of the more technically presented arguments. Schelling's final word on Spinozism, that its error lies in conceiving God's attributes, even God himself, as a *thing*, is tied directly to the absence of *eros* in the discourse. Pantheism, even in its exemplary form, is condemned by its nature to lifelessness and abstractness, since it excludes *eros*. With this, pantheism is also condemned to conceive the whole as well as the parts in terms of thinghood, rather than in terms of living will as nexus of forces.

Another provocation arises with respect to Spinozism. If Spinozism in particular and pantheism in general arises (often) through the liveliest feeling of freedom, how is it that both life (soul) and love are left out of pantheism, so much so that they are conspicuous by their absence? I return to Plato and Kant for clues. In Plato's *Symposium*, Diotima's teaching of Socrates concludes with an ascent from *eros* of beautiful bodies to pure, perfect, disembodied beauty. So entrancing is this prospect that in the very ascent the soul forgets itself as embodied. In so doing, it provides a likeness presenting the forgetfulness of life. Only by the entrance of young and beautiful-bodied Alcibiades is balance restored.

In Kant's *Critique of Practical Reason* the moral law commands "practical love." Practical love is love free of anything "pathological," entirely excluding anything connected with "inclination."[2] This provides an example of how *eros* can come to be excluded from freedom—for the sake of freedom. Both pantheism and practical love reveal the possibility of the self-forgetfulness of the philosopher. Precisely because these philosophical constructions lack the very qualities (liveliness, *eros*) that characterize the soul of the philosopher, a lively and erotic thinker such as Schelling can discern them as the hidden wellspring of these constructions. As he thinks through these constructions, their hidden wellspring is discovered *within* the soul of the philosopher. Thus, this philosophical gaze turns inward, enacting the task set by the Delphic oracle.

Perhaps oddly, these considerations bear directly upon the earlier discussion of logic. Schelling speaks of a "general misunderstanding of the law of identity or the meaning of the copula in judgment" (341), in which there is a failure to note that "in no possible proposition which in the accepted explanation expresses the identity of subject and predicate, a sameness (*Einerleiheit*) or even an immediate connection is expressed" (341). This leads to serious consequences in:

> . . . the higher application of the law of identity: If, for example, the proposition is advanced: the perfect is the imperfect, the meaning is: the imperfect is not through that which and in which it is imperfect, but rather through the perfection in it; for our time, however, it has this meaning: the perfect and the imperfect are the same, everything is equal, the worst and the best, folly and wisdom. (341)

Schelling discloses the source of this misunderstanding in the apparently most harmless of sentences, the logical tautology. He asserts, "The profound logic of the ancients distinguished subject and predicate as antecedent and consequent and thus expressed the real meaning of the law of identity" (342). What *is* "the profound logic of the ancients"? Schelling doesn't say. However, I strongly suggest that the reference is to Heraclitus: "*ouk emou alla tou logou akousantas homologein sophon estin hen panta einai* (listening not to me but to the *logos*, it is wise to agree: one is all)."[3] Schelling's is most certainly a *modern* reading of the fragment, casting it in the language of reason that he inherited from Leibniz and Kant. Other readings, especially Heidegger's, are quite different. However, Schelling's reading conveys the *living* nature of the logical copula. Kant did so as well, ascribing great power to that "*Verhältniswörtchen*" (little word of relation).[4] But Schelling went further, likening the "is" to the principle of sufficient reason. The law of sufficient reason is that law "in virtue of which we believe that no fact can be real or existing and no statement true unless it has a sufficient reason why it should be thus and not otherwise. Most frequently, however, these reasons cannot be known by us."[5] Further,

> Whoever says "a body is a body" is positively *thinking* something different in the subject than in the predicate; by the former the unity, by the latter the particular properties . . . which are related to the unity as *antecedens* is to *consequens*. Just this is the meaning of an older explanation according to which subject and predicate were opposed as enveloped and unfolded (*implicitum et explicitum*). (342)

The misunderstood logic abstracts from the living thought of the thinker and regards the mere proposition as "logic." Acolytes of such formalism forget that a deed (*ergon*) has occurred in any proposition that affirms unity. Without the recollection of the deed of thought, propositions are meaningless, most dramatically those concerning the highest matters such as good and evil.

Schelling's example of tautology "which, if it is not to be altogether meaningless, retains this [living] relationship [of antecedent to consequent]" (342), serves to show the bond of meaning (*Sinn*) to the deed of thinking. Tautology means: "saying of the same." But *tauto* does not mean the merely identical. Schelling's examples show that in order for a tautology to mean anything, that is, "mean" *at all* such that one is even able to recognize it as a tautology, a deed has to occur. Two different thoughts have to be bound together in a single and unified act. Thus, the *tauto* names the gathering of two nonidentical thoughts.

To say the same thing in another way, something crucial and necessary is forgotten in the formalistic logic regarding tautology: namely *logos*, the second element of the word tauto-logy! Here, *logos* simultaneously means gathering into a unity, thinking, and meaning.[6] And since *logos* is forgotten (and thus *tauto* is misconstrued), the act that makes logic possible at all is misconstrued.[7]

Schelling's account of tautology both echoes and enhances Kant's account, which was the first to ascribe a synthetic nature to tautology. A clear exposition of this view is found in a footnote to §15 in the B Edition Transcendental Deduction of the *Critique of Pure Reason*:

> Whether the [combined] representation are in themselves identical, and whether, therefore, one can be analytically thought through the other, is not a question that here arises. The *consciousness* of the one . . . has always to be distinguished from the consciousness of the other; and it is with the synthesis of this possible consciousness that we are here alone concerned. (B130n, emphasis in original)

However, Kant takes pains to separate the law of identity from thc principle of sufficient reason. The law of identity is the necessary but not sufficient condition for knowledge (the *conditio sine qua non*), even though a prior synthesis is required for its formulation. It is merely analytic and therefore able only to indicate the agreement of thought with itself. By contrast, the principle of sufficient reason (*contra* Leibniz) is synthetic through and through. It thereby makes possible knowledge of the empirical manifold by virtue of the pure content it must possess.[8]

By contrast, Schelling takes the bold step of presenting the two as one. They are equally originary (*gleichursprünglich*), most obviously recalling

Leibniz who regarded them as the two most fundamental principles of all. Beyond even this, however, Schelling endows the profound ancient understanding of logic with the laws of reason established by modern philosophy: "The unity of (the law of identity) is an immediately creative unity. Already in the relation of subject to predicate, we have pointed out the relation of ground to consequent, and the law of sufficient reason is therefore just as original a law as the law of identity" (345–46).

The act of *logos*, the deed of articulation, is immediately creative. This means that by virtue of nothing other than itself, *logos* produces or introduces something that was not previously present. *Logos* begets unity in manifoldness. Thus, *logos* and *eros* act simultaneously and are distinguishable only in reflection. However, not only does *logos* as the creative unity of the law of identity bring together what, in Kantian or Aristotelian terms, might be deemed accidents and their subject. The law of identity also brings together diverse laws, indeed the two highest laws of thinking. To say that the law of identity (according to which thinking of whatever kind and content must agree with itself) and the law of sufficient reason are equally originary (*ebenso ursprüngliches*), is to affirm the sameness of identity and nonidentity, of identity and otherness. The law of sufficient reason directs thought backward and forward temporally, in search of antecedent conditions and looking out for future ones. The law of identity directs thought to grasp this succession atemporally, simultaneously. The creative unity of *logos*, in which the two laws are equally originary, thus has the crucial function of fashioning the ground-consequent relation as fundamentally independent of time. Antecedent-consequent does not imply temporal priority. This is why Schelling immediately follows the above-cited words on the law of identity with the remark, "On account of this, the eternal must also be ground immediately, and thus as it is in itself" (346).

This is no mere leap from the finite to the infinite, since the determination of the creative unity of the law of identity arises directly from the closely attentive thinking of the philosopher reflecting on his own deed. It is the thinking of thinking (*reflexio*) that yields the determination of the eternal as immediate ground. That is, in the thinking of thinking the *creative* character of thinking shows itself, in its deed both of introducing something that was not present previously and of discovering the region that makes such creativity possible. In my view, one would speak well if one said that the naming of the eternal as ground is the unfolding of the god outside the philosopher from the god within. The deed of thinking in which a successively apprehended manifold is brought to unity, a deed that occurs nowhere and is bound to no time, is a sign of the eternal as the simultaneous unity.

These reflections prepare the way for the uncovering of freedom as concealed in pantheism. In the simultaneous act of thinking, the consequent is conceived in the ground. The consequent is distinguished from the ground as both not ground and as dependent upon ground for its emergence. This means, "Dependence does not exclude self-subsistence and therefore freedom. It does not determine the essence, and only says that the dependent, whatever it might be, can be only as a consequence of that upon which it depends . . . " (346). Since freedom must be ground (for it could not be grounded in anything else and still be freedom), and the "consequent" of the world unfolds from the ground, the immanence of all things in God (= the world) is thought together with freedom.

However, more than just the possibility of the coexistence of freedom and system may be affirmed. The unfolding of the world through God as free act also follows from the previous developments. In his enhancement of logic that places the law of identity together with law of sufficient reason, and that conceives logic as providing active and creative unity, Schelling is able to infer the real togetherness of freedom and system. "The liveliest feeling of the philosopher," a feeling that leads him/her to construct a pantheistic system, serves as the sign of the nature of their togetherness. It is therefore in light of the physical principle "like to like" that the following remark must be understood:

> The procession (*Folge*) of things from God is a self-revelation of God. God can only become revealed in that which is similar to him, in free beings acting from themselves. . . . If all beings (*Wesen*) in the world were only thoughts of the divine mind, they would have to be living just because of it. (347)

Otherwise, Schelling remarks, God could not find any pleasure (*Lust*). From the system of reason that the philosopher erects to satisfy what is desired from the liveliest feeling of freedom, there is imaged the world-whole that God erects to satisfy the desire for self-revelation. As Schelling seeks the philosopher in the system, God seeks himself in creation. In the eternal act, God speaks and the things are there; the spontaneity of the human understanding is imaged by the eternal act. The ideality of images produced by the human imagination is imaged in the reality of the creatures of the divine imagination.

"The eternal act" means that God is by nature act, rather than a thing that acts. Human thought, itself a creative act that introduces unity, images the divine act of creation. Thus, human thought may be understood as a "derivative absoluteness or divinity (*Göttlichkeit*)" (347). Schelling asserts further, ". . . Such a divinity belongs to nature" (347). The god within finds its likeness therefore in all signs of life, both spiritual and natural. As Schelling wrote, "Insofar as nature is the real aspect of the eternal act by which the subject becomes its own object, the philosophy of nature is the real aspect of philosophy as a whole."[9]

Derivative absoluteness—this has the ring of another contradiction. But Schelling not only denies that there is a contradiction in this notion. He declares, in yet another provocation, that it is "so little a contradiction that it is the central concept of all philosophy" (347). Earlier, Schelling expressed this notion as the immanence in God of all things, and offered formulae such as A/a, A/b, A/c, etc. A/a is reserved for human beings in whom freedom is made fully manifest. The others express natural things. A = Schelling's God = Spinoza's God conceived in terms of freedom. Thus, each individual being is a manifestation of God. And each individual being is free not in spite of but *precisely because of* this immanence.

One peculiarity of humanity's derivative absoluteness is philosophy. The philosophical act of thinking that images and is imaged by the eternal act demonstrates that all thought is primarily *act*. From this primacy, Schelling can speak of the "error in Spinoza's system"; which "does not lie in the circumstance that he posited all things in God, but that they are *things*" (349). From this abstract, lifeless position, Spinoza proceeded "excellently." Thus, the philosopher's reflective discovery of the creative (nonreflective) act of thinking, which discloses the fundamentally creative character of even the most prosaic material connection, has a forceful impact when it encounters Spinozism. The overcoming of Spinozism by means of the ontological distinction of act and thing has the salutary result of raising the central point of philosophy as *creative act* into full relief. Discussing the transformation of his philosophy of nature into a system of reason, Schelling writes:

> In freedom, it was maintained, the final potencifying (*potenzirende*) act is found, through which nature entire transfigures itself into sensation, intelligence, and finally in will.—In the last and highest analysis, there is no other being than willing. Willing is primal being (*Ursein*), and to the latter alone are all its predicates suitable: groundlessness, eternity, independence of time and self-affirmation. All philosophy strives only to find this highest expression. (350)

All four of these predicates came forth in the encounter with pantheism.

To this point, Schelling notes, idealism has elevated philosophy. One hears echoes of the primacy of practical reason in Kant, and of practical reason as identical to the will as "higher faculty of desire." Thus, Kant's critical philosophy achieves the task of placing freedom at its highest point. However, as a complete system, idealism fails to provide sufficient "decision and determinacy" according to Schelling, although it must be credited with supplying the "first complete concept of formal freedom" (351). Because of idealism's accomplishments, the proper investigation of freedom can go forward in spite of its insufficiencies.

The treatment of idealism resembles the treatment of pantheism. Idealism is indispensable for its elevation of freedom. Schelling calls it "the true initiation for the higher philosophy of our time" (351). But like pantheism, idealism is incomplete, and its very incompleteness provides the enticement necessary for its overcoming. Schelling indicates the path to completeness in a way that calls to mind another Heraclitean fragment. He states that systematic completeness demands not only that "activity, life and freedom are alone the truly actual," but that everything actual has as its ground activity, life and freedom. This also calls to mind the Heraclitean "*hodos ano kato mia kai oute*" ("the way up and down is one and the same").[10]

This is so since Schelling makes the following striking claim: "The thought of making freedom once and for all the *one* and *all* of philosophy has liberated (*in Freiheit gesetzt*) the human spirit generally and not merely in relation to itself, and has given science in all its parts a more forceful sudden change than any previous revolution" (351). In this sentence, Schelling presents the synthesis of modern and Greek thought at two of their towering high points, and transcends even this synthesis by ascribing unprecedented living and liberating power to it. This is not merely a synthesis of ideas but a combination of the powerful living acts that gave rise to these ideas in the first place.

I return to the Heraclitean *logos* fragment cited earlier: "*ouk emou alla tou logou akousantas homologein sophon estin hen panta einai*" ("listening not to me but to the *logos*, it is wise to agree: one is all").[11] The *homo-* of the *homologein* is freedom for Schelling. Freedom is thought as the "*hen kai pan*," and the "*pan kai hen*" that are heard in attending to the *logos*. The gathering of all things as well as their differentiation must be seen as freedom and nothing else. Idealism must not only be studied but *undergone* in order to gain sight of freedom in its formal aspect. Nevertheless, idealism provides only the "most general" concept freedom, enough to provoke the *desire* to "make everything over into its analogue (*analog*)" (351), but not enough for the undertaking of this deed. "Mere idealism is not sufficient to show the specific difference, that is, the precise determinateness of *human* freedom" (352).

The philosopher conceives the god outside through the god within, and freedom is the center from which all is to emanate; it is groundless ground. However, the philosopher is human. Therefore, it is necessary to determine what is precisely *human* in human freedom. In pantheism, both freedom and life were concealed. Idealism revealed freedom as the highest point and the source, but life is concealed, more precisely the individuation of reason in actual beings. Life, "the real and living concept of freedom," must come forth, as pervading the ideal (formal) and general. Schelling asserts: Freedom in the real and living sense is "a capacity for good and evil" (352). Thus, the presence of good and evil in the philosopher must serve as the sign of freedom. Schelling has said, however, that the philosopher is the one who keeps the understanding pure and undarkened by evil. What can be made of this provocation? Clearly, good and evil are co-present in human beings, and for Schelling their strife provokes the recognition of human freedom, that is, of freedom individualized, that is, of living freedom. While the philosopher is certainly given over to that strife in ways that will become clear as the *Freedom Essay* progresses, the philosopher's task is to keep the *understanding* (*Verstand*) pure and undarkened by evil.

Simply stated, evil is necessary for the disclosure of freedom: no evil, no freedom. Yet the presence of evil in God is impossible. This is not maintained on faith in divine goodness but precisely on account of the demand for system. To say that both good and evil are admitted is to say that a fundamental duality reigns that by its very nature cannot be overcome. Ultimately, this means all science would be impossible. The duality would mock all attempts at unity of any kind. And yet, either good and evil are both admitted, or freedom is excluded. If freedom were excluded, any pretensions of human beings with respect to any activity of any kind, especially moral activity, would be rendered ludicrous.

Schelling works through the classical attempts to make the origin of evil intelligible as co-present with God yet not caused by the first cause (353–56), showing how each either fails to explain the reality of evil (evil as a privation of good, and nothing in itself), or fails to account for good (introducing pandaemonism instead of pantheism, that is, total fragmentation, the despair of reason). He then indicates why such attempts must fall short on account of their one-sidedness:

> Idealism, if it does not preserve a living realism as a basis, becomes as empty and abstract a system as the Leibnizian, Spinozist or any other dogmatic system. All neo-European philosophy since its beginning

> (through Descartes) has this common lack, that nature is not present for it and that it lacks the living ground to it . . . idealism is the soul of philosophy, realism is its body; only both together constitute a living whole. Realism can never supply the principle, but must be ground and means wherein the former actualizes itself, takes on flesh and blood. (356)

The task of solving the problem of evil is the task of conceiving and articulating a living god. The withdrawal of nature from neo-European philosophy brought with it the removal of God from the world, and thus made the problem of the origin of evil nearly impossible to encounter: "The abhorrence (*Abscheu*) against anything real, which might impurify (*verunreinigen*) the spiritual with each touch, must naturally make blind the sight seeking for the origin of evil" (356). What is required, then, is a god of flesh and blood, a god willing to get dirty. Needed is a god undergoing life, and this means a god who undergoes death. The conception of a finite god accomplishes the following: (1) it unites the soul and body, (2) it makes the co-presence of good and evil intelligible, (3) it accounts for the oneness of freedom and system, and (4) it makes manifest the contradiction of freedom and necessity that animates all higher activities of the spirit.

Schelling closes his introductory remarks by implicitly likening the ideal principle, the unifying principle "of reason and science" to the masculine, and the real mediating basis or ground, by implication, to the feminine. The need of the ideal principle (reason, unity, the immediate simultaneous act) to find a living basis (the real, individuating, mediating ground) images the erotic togetherness of male and female. Thus, the introduction ends with the suggestion of *eros*, bringing differing natures to unity . . . on the earth.

> (

The Account of the Possibility of Evil

HAVING CLEARED THE WAY for the investigations proper by "the correction of essential concepts" (357), Schelling begins by calling upon his own philosophy of nature to provide the point of departure for the unfolding of the essence of human freedom. Schelling's philosophy of nature seeks to put to rest the general view that nature lacks spirit (*Geist*)—living reason. Instead, nature is a manifestation of life and a "derivative absolute" (347), an image of the whole as such. It contains within it all that is needed for the unfolding of the whole. By working through nature upward to reason, the presence of reason in nature is made manifest. Light and gravity, the principles of nature, are unified and distinguished at once. This same simultaneous unification and distinction occurs for the sake of the principles of intelligence, including highest intelligence. Just as nature is the symbol of God, God is symbolized by nature. "The real side of that eternal act becomes manifest in nature; nature in itself, or eternal nature, is precisely spirit born into the objective. . . ."[1]

Schelling writes: "The philosophy of nature of our time has established the distinction in science for the first time between essence (*Wesen*) insofar as it exists, and essence insofar as it is the ground of existence" (357). Several related earlier writings are referenced in the Gutmann translation of the *Freedom Essay*.[2] I reproduce the most directly germane among them, all from *Darstellung meines Systems der Philosophie* (*Presentation of my System of Philosophy*) (1801) in which Schelling's philosophy of nature is expounded in a more finished form than in his 1797 *Ideen zu einer Philosophie der Natur* (*Ideas toward a Philosophy of Nature*). The "*meines*" distinguishes the Schellingian system based upon "production" from the Fichtean system based upon "reflection."[3] After discoursing upon their difference and declaring that he would follow the model of Spinoza (for Schelling, the quintessential "realist" and the only truly nondualistic thinker), he closes his "Preface" (*Vorerinnerung*) with the words: "From now on only the matter itself speaks" (*Von jetzt an spreche nur die Sache selbst*).[4]

> Absolute identity is the immediate ground of *primum Existens* not in itself, but rather through A and B which are equivalent (*gleich*) to it.—On the other hand the absolute identity is absolutely-immediately and *in itself* ground of the *being-real* of A and B, but just on account of that, absolute identity *is* not yet in gravity. [This is so] because the absolute identity exists (*ist*) only (in gravity) after A and B are posited as existing (*seiend*). And precisely on account of this, gravity is posited immediately through absolute identity and follows not (only) from its essence, also not from its actual *being* (because this is not yet posited), but rather (from its essence insofar as it proceeds to its being, therefore) from its *nature*, from which however it follows absolutely and immediately out of its inner necessity, namely from the fact that it is unconditioned, and cannot be except under the form of (the equivalent) being of A and B. (Out of the *immediate* being-posited of gravity through absolute identity) it becomes evident how impossible it would be to ground gravity as gravity or present it in actuality, since it must be thought as absolute identity, not insofar as the latter is, but rather insofar as it is the ground of its own being, and therefore not itself in actuality.[5]

In this passage, the ground/existence unity/twofold is spoken about in terms of absolute identity and gravity. Neither can *be* without the other. They are distinguishable only in *logos*. However, their belonging together in actuality as *one* follows from an inner necessity. The ground/existence distinction in the *Freedom Essay* images the absolute identity/gravity distinction in the *Darstellung*.

> In gravity we must indeed recognize absolute identity according to its essence, but not as e x i s t i n g (*s e i e n d*)[6] since it is rather the ground of its being (itself) in its essence (*in jener*). . . . Absolute identity itself goes into the light and into actuality. Gravity flees into the eternal night, and absolute identity itself does not completely dissolve the seal under which it lies bound, although it is forced to come forth under the potency of A and B, however as the One Identical and as it were, into the light.[7]

This passage anticipates the ground/existence distinction in another way of imaging. *Light* and *night* come forth as ways of bringing forth the ground/existence unity/twofold. This bringing forth as the One Identical (*das Eine Identische*) anticipates the imaging in the *Freedom Essay* in which Schelling declares the necessary togetherness of God and ground in terms of their merely "reflective" distinguishability.

> We understand by nature absolute identity in general, insofar as it is considered not as existing, but rather as ground of its being, and we here foresee that we will name everything nature which lies beyond the absolute being of absolute identity.[8]

In this third passage, absolute identity is called *ground*. This image, of course, constitutes a wellspring of Schelling's thought in the *Freedom Essay*.

The affirmation of the twofoldness inherent in the whole belongs to all three passages. As has been shown, nature for Schelling is nothing distinct from thinking or intelligence, and must be understood in its unity with the latter. Nature is not *being* over against *knowing*. Rather, nature is precisely what is known in knowing. It is the objective dimension of the primordial unity of subjective and objective. Conceived as nature, subject-objectivity is understood as absolute identity or light, and gravity. The mutual needfulness of the two is spoken of as absolute identity or light as its own ground and as self-contained cause of itself, but not as existing, not as actual. Absolute identity (light) comes to be actual only insofar as it is bound to gravity (darkness, chaos, matter). Gravity grounds the light while not itself possessing itself any ground. As indicated in the passages cited above, the twofold of light and gravity is separable in speech only. In nature, this twofold occurs in their essential togetherness. Gravity must be thought as *grounding* without ground, and absolute identity as the intelligible principle must be thought as *ground* in need of grounding. Absolute identity is real only insofar as it occurs in actuality, together with gravity as its necessary other. In the same way, gravity owes its determinate existence to absolute identity, and could not be at all without the latter.

I suggest strongly that these remarks, which at once gather the logical reflections of the Introduction and foreshadow the remainder of the *Freedom Essay*, should be grasped in two simultaneous and related senses. The first sense concerns their adumbration of the ground/existence distinction that provides an ontological account of the possibility of evil. The inseparability of the principles of light and darkness in God images their separability in man. This separabilty accounts for the possibility of human freedom which, as precisely coextensive with the ascendance of the dark principle, is at once the possibility of positive evil. The second concerns the emergence of this crucial ontological distinction out of Schelling's ongoing dialogue with and visceral response to the high points in the philosophy of the chronological past. In his gathering of ancient and modern, Schelling thinks the foundations of modern scientific reason together with the mythical character of Greek thinking. Although the remarks seem opaque upon first reading, this meeting of ancient and modern in them serves as a way of entry into this most provocative thinker, into the work that even Hegel, who had become a philosophical adversary by 1809, considered "profound and speculative."[9] As the *Freedom Essay* is an account issuing simultaneously from a mythical as well as a rational source, the unfolding of the distinction of ground and existence for the sake of the problem of evil (the problem of freedom) is, therefore, also a conversation with the history of philosophy.

Although the ground/existence distinction is philosophically original with Schelling, one can trace a path to it in Kant's *Critique of Pure Reason*. Schelling will transform it, but Kant planted its dialogical seed. I return to the split between the law of identity and the law of sufficient reason discussed above. Whereas the law of identity is the law of all thinking regardless of the matter thought, "the principle of sufficient reason is . . . the ground of possible experience, that is of objective knowledge of appearances in respect to their relation in the order of time" (A201, B246). And since nature is nothing but "synthetic unity of the manifold of appearances according to rules" (A126–27) whose laws the *understanding* provides, the principle of sufficient reason, comprehended through the category of causality, is the ground of nature.

This view effects the separation of the two principles in the understanding, but even more significantly it effects the separation between thought (as thought of an object), on the one hand, and existence, on the other. The character of this separation is most strikingly presented in the "Ideal of Pure Reason," concerning Kant's critique of the ontological proof for the existence of God. This section is especially germane to the ground–existence distinction in Schelling. Even in the face of this devastating critique by Kant, Schelling maintained that the ontological proof of the reality of God is "a remnant of genuine philosophy."[10]

For Kant, the ontological proof in all its forms rests upon the confounding of a real with a logical predicate. A logical predicate merely asserts the relation of a predicate to a subject, for example "all bachelors are unmarried," or "some unicorns are cone-headed animals." By contrasts, real predicates assert a distinguishing mark that can be found in the object, for which the concept of the subject serves as a rule, for example, "some apples are green." Granting that the concept of God includes the predicate of perfection, the latter predicate is merely *logical.* No actual distinguishing mark, such as real *existence*, can be inferred from this merely logical predicate. Thus, the inference from the possibility of the concept of God to the existence of God (from the predicate of perfection, implying existence) unlawfully jumps the gap between logical unity (ruled by the law of identity) and the unity of possible experience.

> It is not therefore surprising that, if we attempt to think existence through the pure category alone, we cannot discern a single mark distinguishing it from mere possibility. (A601, B629)

Judgments of existence, which entail the actual presence of an object outside its concept, requires something more:

> Whatever, therefore, and however much, our concept of an object may contain, we must go outside it, if we are to ascribe existence to the object. In the case of objects of the senses, this takes place through their connection with some one of our perceptions in accordance with empirical laws. But in dealing with objects of pure thought, we have no means whatsoever of knowing their existence. . . . (A601, B629)

The gulf between thought and existence clearly cannot be bridged by mere formal logic. In Kant's transcendental logic, the pure concepts of the understanding gain objective reality through their being limited by a condition at once sensible and transcendental: the pure intuition of time. The categories provide the rules for the synthesis of the sensible manifold in time. The schemata (which require far more discussion than is possible here[11]) are the procedures of productive imagination that make it possible for the rules to rule. The schemata do the ruling, and in doing provide the categories with *significance* (*Bedeutung*) (A146, B185). Pure intuition is both ruled by the categories and schemata, and limits the scope of their rule. The three elements, taken together, become principles (*Grundsätze*), rules for appearances in time.

However, this limiting can be looked at as a compromise. When it is limited, the understanding does not surrender its spontaneity. Rather, its character as immediate lawgiver is given a domain in which its rule is secured. That is, the understanding remains (by virtue of its connection with the schemata of imagination) *creative*:

> The manner in which something is apprehended in appearance can be so determined *a priori* that the rule of synthesis can at once give, that is to say *bring into being*, this element of *a priori* intuition in every example that comes before us empirically. The *existence* of appearances cannot, however, be known *a priori*; and even granting that we could in any such manner contrive to infer that something exists, we could not know it determinately. . . . (A178, B221)

In "exchange" for foregoing immediate contact with existence, the understanding is granted the power to introduce order into the chaos of appearances. In this limited but highly significant sense, human thought for Kant can be read as a creative deed by its nature.

However, pure thought in general, as distinguished from pure thought of an object in general (a distinction that, as we shall see, takes place only in *logos*), hardly drops out of consideration. Nor does the principle of contradiction (the law of identity) serve as merely "the universal, though merely negative condition of our judgments in general."[12] In the Transcendental Dialectic, its role as a necessary but not sufficient criterion of truth is preserved but recast. "Mere" logical possibility moves to the center of the problematic in Kant's solution to the Third Antinomy, the antinomy of freedom and necessity. As we have seen, Kant takes great care to restrict his solution to the evidence at hand. Accordingly, he expressly denies proving the possibility of freedom, "since we cannot from mere concepts *a priori* know the possibility of any real ground and its causality" (A558, B586). He can only claim that causality through freedom *does not contradict* natural causality.

This suggests that the two laws of the understanding, the law of identity and the law of causality (i.e., of sufficient reason), are in the final analysis united after a fashion in human cognition. Looked upon from a more encompassing perspective, the two laws cleave with respect to the whole. The law of causality, ruling pure intuition through its schema, restricts knowledge to appearances. The law of identity opens out into the realm of practical freedom in the *Critique of Practical Reason*, where rational belief (rational faith) provides access to the ideas of reason (God, the soul, the world) that were inaccessible by means of knowledge.

The schematized categories are *constitutive* of experience, unifying the manifold of intuition in the understanding. The ideas of reason are regulative, bringing the manifold of knowledge in the understanding to ever-greater unity. The ideas of reason can serve as *regulative* principles because they admit of being *thought together with* the empirical manifold according to the law of identity. Thus, we can understand how Schelling, sparked by such a reading of Kant, affirmed the equiprimordiality of the two laws. The *hen panta*, the unity of the system, therefore, requires that the law of identity assume a central position.

Kant's employment of the law of identity comes about rather subtly, and Schelling incorporates it with similar subtlety. The law of identity as *conditio sine qua non* rules all thought irrespective of content, and this also means irrespective of *time*.

> Pure reason, as a purely intelligible faculty, is not subject to the form of time, nor consequently to the conditions of succession of time. The causality of reason in its intelligible character does not, in producing an effect, *arise* or begin to be at a certain time. For in that case it would itself be subject to the natural law of appearances, in accordance with which the causal series are determined in time; and its causality would then be nature, not freedom. (A551–52, B579–80)

In the Analytic of the *Critique of Pure Reason*, independence of time disqualified general (pure formal) logic from serving as a positive determinant of experiential knowledge. In the Dialectic, however, independence of time qualifies this same law to open the way beyond the empirical manifold to the practical realm.

Schelling's thought of the identity and equivalent originariness (*Gleichursprünglichkeit*) of the law of identity and the law of sufficient reason is, therefore, a daring but entirely justified interpretation-transformation of Kant's. Both laws originate from the self-identical pure reason. Both laws simultaneously address reason's relation both to itself and to objects. Still further, one can appreciate how this cleaving is creative, bringing together that which rules the temporal (law of sufficient reason) and that which rules the eternal (in the *Critique of Pure Reason*, however, this is thought negatively, as independence of time). It remains to be shown how, starting from Kant, a path to the ground/existence distinction may be drawn. Still more, why is the drawing of such a path crucial to the distinctive nature of Schelling's thought?

For with all of this, the outcome of the Kantian philosophy is the sundering of ground from existence. Whether one speaks of the ground of nature (the principle of sufficient reason) or the ground of human action (freedom and the moral law), the fact remains that the ground falls on the side of thought (intelligibility) and existence remains something outside. A strong indication of the path occurs in the early work of Schelling, in which his thought moves from a reflective character (within the limits of Fichte's *Wissenschaftslehre*, in which that author provocatively and, for German Idealism, decisively recasts the Kantian philosophy) to a "speculative" character. This movement is expressed quite succinctly in the 1796–1797 writings, *Abhandlungen zur Erläuterung des Idealismus der Wissenschaftslehre*. Naming the self-conscious I "spirit," he writes:

> . . . Spirit, insofar as it intuits objects *in general*, intuits itself. If this can be proven, the reality of our knowledge is certain.
> It may be asked, "How is this done?"
> First of all it is necessary that one take possession of that standpoint at which subject and object in us, intuition and intuited, are *identical*. This can occur only through a free act.
> Further: I call *spirit* only that which is *its own* object. Spirit is to be object *for itself*, not however insofar as it is originally *object*, but rather insofar as it is *absolute subject*, for which everything (including itself) is *object*. Thus it must also be. Object is something *dead*, something resting which is capable itself of no *self-activity*, which is merely opposed (G e g e n s t a n d) to act. Spirit, however, can only be grasped *in its activity* . . . ; it is, therefore, only in *becoming*, or rather it is itself nothing other than an *eternal becoming*.[13]

According to this passage, all apprehension of objects is living, spiritual apprehension. Those entities that are called "real objects" and to which "existence" is ascribed are not original. Rather, they are secondary manifestations of spirit as *act*, which is their original. Thus, the split between ground and existence is only apparent. It occurs only at the phenomenal level. At the highest level there is only act, free of all limitation and determination, infinite in the sense of unbounded. Being, in this regard, means finitude. It is a limitation of act within act. However, spirit, as at once self-active and object for itself, is at once infinite and finite. Thus Schelling writes: "Spirit is therefore . . . neither finite nor infinite, but rather in it is the original *unification of finite and infinite* (a new determination of the spiritual character.)"[14]

Thus, there is a significant dimension of the ground/existence distinction that can be traced to Kant. The ground is *thinking as act*: the spontaneity of the understanding as it produces order in the manifold of appearances (principle of sufficient reason—*Satz vom Grund*), and as providing the intelligibility of the moral law, which is ground for human action as self-determination. Further, neither Kant nor Schelling held that our knowledge of objects contained knowledge of their original essence. However, where Kant conceives existence as somehow *given* externally, Schelling understands existence as nothing other than the *self*-externalization of spirit. In this way, the ground/existence distinction does not imply a duality of principles (for ground and existence are originally the same) but merely a distinction within the self-same spirit, contained within the same act of knowing itself. Ground and existence are distinguishable, but only in *logos*.

Yet this answer is only a partial one. It is an *idealistic* answer, and therefore one-sided. It makes manifest the unity of ground and existence, but not their specific difference. Nor is the character of the finitude–infinitude of spirit made manifest at all. To the account in the *Abhandlungen* there must be added another. In the *Critique of Pure Reason* nature may be said *not to be present* in the sense that only through thought (the understanding as law-giver of nature) can nature even come about. Since thought is a means, nature is manifest only mediately. In other words, an abstraction has been made from nature as living.

Using the language of the 1798–1799 *Abhandlungen*, the life of nature is not immediately present but present only as a consequence, that is, as a result of spirit's self-knowing. But nature must be present in a *living* ground. There may be a sense in which the life of nature is expression and symbol of the free act of spirit. Nevertheless, the presence of nature from out of *itself* has not been articulated. In other words, the unity of ground and existence is more than the homogeneity of spirit with itself in its deepest sense. If this were merely this homogeneity, then the unity of the law of identity with the law of sufficient reason would not be creative but merely reflective.

A clue to the deeper sense is available in the "new determination of the spiritual character" as the unification of infinitude and finitude, without being either. A most peculiar and provocative unification! It is not enough to unfold the character of spirit as act and as life-source. The origin of spirit *beyond* finitude and infinitude must somehow be thought and expressed. Since the essence of human freedom is "the capability of good and evil" and a posture somehow beyond infinitude and finitude is required, one is provoked to wonder: Where and how can one stand in order to take such a posture? How can it be shown?

But in the *Abhandlungen*, spirit *is* an origin. One cannot go behind it in order to provide a proof in the sense of a rational demonstration. However, another kind of demonstration is available. This kind, too, emerges from the dialogue with ancient philosophy. In modern thought "apodeictic," from the Greek *apodeixis*, means "absolutely certain," and is reserved primarily for mathematical matters. For example, of space and time, and especially of the former, Kant writes:

> It is evident that in regard to both [space and time] there is a large number of *a priori* apodeictic and synthetic propositions. This is especially true of space. . . . Since the propositions of geometry are known with apodeictic certainty. (A46–47, B64)

This reading of *apodeixis* closes off access to any notion of the infinite and the finite that is neither. But in Greek thought, *apodeixis* can have another and quite different sense.

It has such a sense at a turning point in Plato's *Phaedrus*, a dialogue of *eros*. Precisely after his discourse on the forms of divine madness and before beginning his palinode to *eros*, Socrates says the following to Phaedrus: "*he de de estai deinois men apistos . . . sophois de piste . . . arkhe de apodeixeos hede* (the clever will not trust this demonstration [or 'proof'], but the wise will trust it. . . . The demonstration begins as follows)" (245c1–2, 4). Socrates then gives a mythical speech, in which he presents the ascent of the mortal soul to a place that it can glimpse the divine banquet where the gods feast on "*ousia ontos ousa* (being beingly being)" (247c9). Mythological speaking, therefore, must reenter philosophy. As it is bound neither to finitude nor to infinitude, mythological speaking allows finite and infinite to meet across this supposedly impassable gulf. The path from Kant to the ground/existence distinction, then, passes perhaps strangely through Plato. In this way, the thought of the philosopher is at once a recollection of the history of philosophy. As this history serves the recovery of a living ground, the history of philosophy is a *living* history.

Plato's *Timaeus* plays a special role in Schelling's thought.[15] Some of its key passages provide the needed transition from Kant's conception of ground to Schelling's treatment of it by way of myth. Socrates and Timaeus acknowledge their mortal natures and the consequent status of human *logos* limits occurs at the outset of Timaeus' discourse by appealing to the gods:

> Socrates: Since after this, the task of speaking (*ergon legein*) belongs to you, you might call upon the gods, according to custom.
>
> Timaeus: But Socrates, anyone with any sense of moderation (*sophrosunes*) will always call upon a god before setting out on any venture, whatever its importance.

> In our case, we are about to make (*poieisthai*) speeches about the universe, whether it has an origin or even if it does not, and so if we're not going to go astray it is necessary to call upon the gods and goddesses, and pray that they approve of all that we have to say, as we will too. (27b7–d1)

The need for mythical speaking is expressly acknowledged in what follows:

> Now that which is created must, as we say, of necessity be created by some cause. But the creator and father of the whole is past finding out, and if we found him we would be incapable of the deed of speaking to all about it: So therefore we must examine this, namely which of the paradigms the artificer worked from. . . . (28c2–29a1)

The origin of the whole remains both withdrawn and inaccessible to *logos*. However, the act of the father must be examined. Thus, the task of human speech here is to bring forth the nature of the deed without being able to account for its "doer." Speech (*logos*) is bound to deed (*ergon*), since creation as act is accessible to human beings at least in some way. That is, in some way the ascent from what is present to the paradigms of what is present can be made. Timaeus cites what might loosely be called the "principle" of this "in some way" for the ascent in *logos*:

> Above all the origin of all should originate according to nature. And in speaking of the image and the paradigm we must determine that the words show (*exegetai*) that they are akin to the matters they are concerned with: when they show the abiding and secure and intelligible (*meta nou*) they ought to be clearly abiding and unchanging . . . and as far as possible irrefutable and invincible, and it is necessary that they be nothing less—but when they give a likeness of the latter, they need only be likely or analogous (*ana logon*) to the former words. . . . Enough if we produce accounts as likely as any other, for we must remember (*memnemenous*) that I who am the speaker and you who are the judges are mortal men by nature, and we ought to accept a likely myth (*eikota muthon*) and seek no further. (29b2–d3)

Human speech as human and therefore as mortal, as both generated and passing away, cannot by its nature speak directly of the eternal paradigms. Nor can human speech claim intelligibility (*nous*) as such. Timaeus's words acknowledge the bond of human speech to imagery. Insofar as images of the paradigms are accessible to human beings, speech most appropriately images these paradigms as it *images their images*. When the claim is made that *logos* presents the eternal paradigms as they are in truth, the limits of human speech are transgressed (*hubris*). Therefore, the presentation of the ascent in speech to the eternal paradigms must always be understood as a *likely account*.

The closing remark in the prior passage, that we ought to accept a likely myth (*eikota muthon*) and seek no further, affirms the limits of human knowledge within which all *logos* must hold itself. The command to recollect (*memnemenous*) the human character of the speakers of the dialogue establishes that the proper deed of the human soul is recollection rather than original creation. By observing this limit, human speech gives itself the space to speak creatively in a manner suitable to its nature. For the paradigms are present in all seeing though not directly given. It falls to human speech to bring forth these paradigms, to uncover them without violation.

However, if the origin of the whole is inaccessible to *logos* and the presentation of the paradigms in *logos* cannot take place according to *nous* as such, how can the "principle" of production be presented in *logos*? Still further, how is the speaking of this principle to be measured? Since the father (origin) is inaccessible, and the father is said to be the cause (*aitios*), then the "principle" cannot be accounted for in terms of direct causality. Human speech is not capable of such an account. Rather, the "principle" must be spoken of in terms of an *imaging* of the origin if it is to be appropriate to the nature of human speech.

The "principle" of imaging (which, of course, is no rational principle at all), is not aimed at truth in the sense of an entirely adequate representation of the original. Rather, it is *beauty* in the sense of the shining forth of the origin in an image. As the shining forth of being, it is a *vicarious* image that provokes the participation of the seer in what is imaged in the image. Timaeus speaks in this way of the "principle" of beauty: ". . . (the creator) thought that like (*homoion*) is incalculably (*homoiotaton*) more beautiful (*kallion*) than unlike (*anomoiou*)" (33b6–7). "Like to like" therefore characterizes both the way the world was fashioned, and the way the paradigms are imaged in and by the visible things in which they are at once present and withdrawn. Still further, the presenting of beautiful images in speech calls forth a likeness (beautiful image) of themselves in those who hear. Thus "like to like" gathers many key themes of the *Timaeus*. It accounts for the joining of the human to the divine in the presentation of the togetherness of *logos* and *eros*, which produces unity within the limits of human speech. It accounts for the image of the divine as *poietikos* (poet, maker), mirroring the limited but real human creativity to which we do have access. Finally, it speaks to the way of showing in *logos*: the shining of being (beauty) is to be sought in the gathering of like to like, within which the human being who hears appropriately also comes to shine.

Thus, the ground/existence distinction in Schelling's work will come to be heard appropriately in terms of the speaking of the *Timaeus*. The absence of nature as living presence for the Kantian philosophy is not so much an indictment of modern thought for its failure to *conceive* a living basis for nature. Rather, since *nature as living* is prior to any concept, the very conceptual speaking that characterizes modern philosophy closes itself off from life. Conceptual thinking is *abstract*. Such speaking severs itself from the aforementioned vicarious image. With respect both to knowledge and to action, the Kantian philosophy requires distance from the beautiful understood as that which entices. In the *Critique of Judgment*, the beautiful occurs only as subjective agreement of the cognitive faculties. In the *Critique of Practical Reason*, as we have seen, love is not *eros* in the sense of a longing response to an enticement but "practical love," love "commanded" by the moral law. In a certain sense, there is also a purification from *life* required by the Kantian philosophy. Also in the *Critique of Practical Reason*, Kant speaks of "a respect for something entirely different from life, in comparison and contrast to which life and its enjoyment have absolutely no worth."[16]

This severance from life must not be understood as a blunder of any sort. Rather, it must be understood as the necessary consequence of a critique of pure reason by pure reason, for which language serves only as reason's self-articulation. The mythologizing of reason for Schelling is, therefore, most fundamentally a reinterpretation of *logos*. It is a recollection of *logos* as unifying what is diverse and as making nature present in the appropriate manner, that is, nature as living, shown as such in an image.

It is, therefore, no accident that the first account of creation, made in terms of the ground/existence distinction, calls the *Timaeus* of Plato back to mind. The split within the simultaneity of the creative deed between *nous* and *anagke* (the receptacle)[17] closely resembles the split between ground and that in which ground shows itself (existence). The unification of modern pantheism (realism) with modern idealism will take place, and can only take place, as a recollection of the Greeks.

❧

The first account is divided into two parts, the first of which (from God) is very brief, the second (from things) rather longer. The first presents the twofold within God: God viewed absolutely, that is, God as existing, and the ground of God's existence. To be sure, God contains within himself the ground of his existence.[18] But other philosophers have failed to distinguish God from the ground. "This ground of his existence, which God contains in himself, is not God considered absolutely, that is, insofar as he exists. Rather it is the ground of his existence, it is *nature*—in God. The ground is indivisible from him to be sure, but nevertheless distinguishable" (358). The distinguishability occurs in speech and not in deed. The act of creation, occurring all at once, does not have any "prior" or "subsequent" with respect to time. "There is here no first and no last, because everything reciprocally is presupposed, nothing is the other yet nothing is without the other" (358). Thus, in one sense, the ground precedes God as existing, and, in another, God precedes the ground insofar as otherwise the ground would not be ground. Since philosophy concerns itself with the character of the whole as pervading the parts, the first account of the whole indicates the character of this pervasiveness as simultaneity of part and whole. Further, since the ground is "real and actual," and since a reciprocal needfulness of God and ground is implied, the act of creation (the whole as act) may itself be seen as an act rooted in *need*. God himself, *lacking* nature, *needs* nature. This need is imaged in the need of philosophy for system, a need provoked by the philosopher's living feeling of freedom. That is, the need intrinsic to the deed of creation is a vicarious image of the philosopher's deed of *logos*. The binding in speech of present and absent in the likely account is mirrored in the binding of god and his living ground in creation. Thus, the "principle" of "like to like," according to which the philosopher grasps the god outside him, is at once the "principle" according to which the image of God in speech is formed.

The consideration from things up to God brings this forth even more closely to our human stance. Each individual thing is, in a certain regard, an image of the whole.[19] It falls to human beings to grasp wholes through individual "cases." Schelling states the "contradiction": The concept of becoming, since it is a living concept, is the only one appropriate to things. But since there is no becoming in God, things would be absolutely distinct from God. Yet there can be nothing outside God. "This contradiction can only be solved by things having their ground in that *in* God which is *not* God himself" (359, emphases mine). Thus, the very existence of things in time (nature and life), points to a contradiction in the conception of the whole as simultaneous unity.

One might here think of Plato's *Republic* VII, and regard this contradiction as a modern instance of one of those opposites that "summon the intellect" (523b). Thinking is thus impelled upward to account for the contradiction. The ground/existence distinction considered in this regard emerges out of the need of thought both (1) to agree with itself, and (2) to agree with what it thinks. It supplies an image both of the requisite unity and of distinction and differentiation. As Schelling mentions in a footnote: "This is the only correct dualism, namely one which *at the same time* allows a unity" (359n).

In one of the decisive passages in the *Freedom Essay*, one which may seem minor, a mere "figure of speech," Schelling discloses the nature of *logos* for man, and at the same time the nature of his own speech in the *Freedom Essay*: "If we wanted to (*Wollen wir uns*) bring this being (*Wesen*) nearer to us in a human fashion, we can say (*so können wir sagen*) . . ." (359). The antecedent speaks of *will*, more precisely will that wills in an appropriately human way. The task of bringing the divine into the neighborhood of man may be accomplished by the act of willing in an appropriate way. The consequent characterizes this act as a *saying*, rooted in our ability to speak (*sagen können*). In other words, *logos* is given to man so that through it (dialectic) we may bring near that which is present throughout all yet concealed from view. The creative, poetic character of *logos* is, therefore, not a bringing forth in the sense of original production but a bringing near of that which is always present but also easily forgotten.

Logos, tied to the will that wants the nearness of the gods, is at once tied to this recollection. In recognizing the gap between the human and the divine in our *logoi*, we are able to speak in such a way that what we say is both a humanly produced image (generated, given over to becoming) and a divine image (ungenerated, eternal Being): "It is the longing which the eternal One feels to give birth to itself" (359). The account of creation is, therefore, at once an account of the coming to life of God. One can also call it the unfolding of the distinction of ground and existence for the sake of the problem of evil, and, therefore, also discloses the essence of human freedom. The same account presents the unity of freedom and system.

In this unity, far more is at stake than the intelligibility of freedom in its conjunction with system. Intelligibility itself is included in the tale. The account indeed presents an explanation with which "the facts of the matter" can accord. All the matters heretofore mentioned find a place within the account. But more significantly, the account is a *vicarious image of the living whole*. The human being can see himself reflected in a beautiful image. At the same time, since it is an image, and since this image occurs in a tale (*muthos*), the image—just as the human being—remains within proper measure.

The image of God before creation is drawn in terms of will (longing, desire) and understanding (intelligibility, universalization and differentiation), which are divisible only in *logos*. ("Understanding is actually the will in willing" [359].) These are also called "dark" and "light" principles. Just as nothing can be seen in pure darkness, so nothing can be seen in pure light. One needs the other, indeed each is for the sake of the other if anything is to show itself at all, and both are needed preeminently for God to see himself in an image. The act of creation, or the birth of God, must, therefore, be accounted for out of a twofoldness *in* God. The two "folds" are nothing outside the timeless single deed in which God comes to self-manifestation. Nevertheless, these folds must be distinct in order for there to be anything revealed at all.[20] Figure 3.1 provides an outline of the first account, which seeks only to present the progress of the account in an abstract fashion.[21]

The following comments refer to the chart, which merely provides an overview. The comments are intended to flesh out and animate the abstract presentation.

1. The right side of the chart, when completed, will present spirit (the living unity of ground and existence) as history. The reason for its absence at this point is not that the task of the first account is to present the creative deed as simultaneous, therefore excluding considerations of time. History could indeed be presented on the chart as simultaneous. It would have had to be so presented, since the chart presents creation from the standpoint of God. There is just as little problem conceiving the successive in nature simultaneously as there is in conceiving the successive in history. The reason history is not yet broached is that the task of the section concerns only the *exhibition* of the possibility of evil. That is, the account has to make comprehensible only the divisibility of the principles in man.

2. Despite its abstractness, the diagram unmistakably shows the equiprimordiality of Ground and Existence. However, equiprimordiality does not imply equality or equivalence. In this aspect, the *Freedom Essay* moves beyond his earlier formulations in the *Darstellung* cited above, which anticipates the decisive distinction but in which the radical notion of the unruly does not surface:

> Following the eternal act of self-revelation, the world as we now behold it is all rule, order, and form; but the unruly (*das Regellose*) lies ever in the depths as though it might again break through, and order and form nowhere appear to be the original (*das Ursprüngliche*), but it seems as

First Account of Creation
(with respect to nature)
Ground
Will
Longing
Unruly
Darkness
God's ground
Plato's "Matter"
Existence
Understanding
Unity
Rule, Order, and Form
Light
God himself
God's reflexive representation
Spirit
(Word)
Ground/Existence
(nature)
Chaos, depths in which God's essence is locked away (light of life)
Disclosure of hidden unity (in light)—*Ein-bilden*
Division of Forces
Individuated Beings
Divided forces
(body)
Center of division
(soul)
Twofold principle of each
Ground
(light concealed in ground)
Self-will
Particular Will
Consonant
Light
(ground revealed in light)
Primal Will
Universal Will
Vowel
Spirit
(Selfhood—Personality)
Unity of light and dark
(Nature—Creature)
Light
(God—primal will)

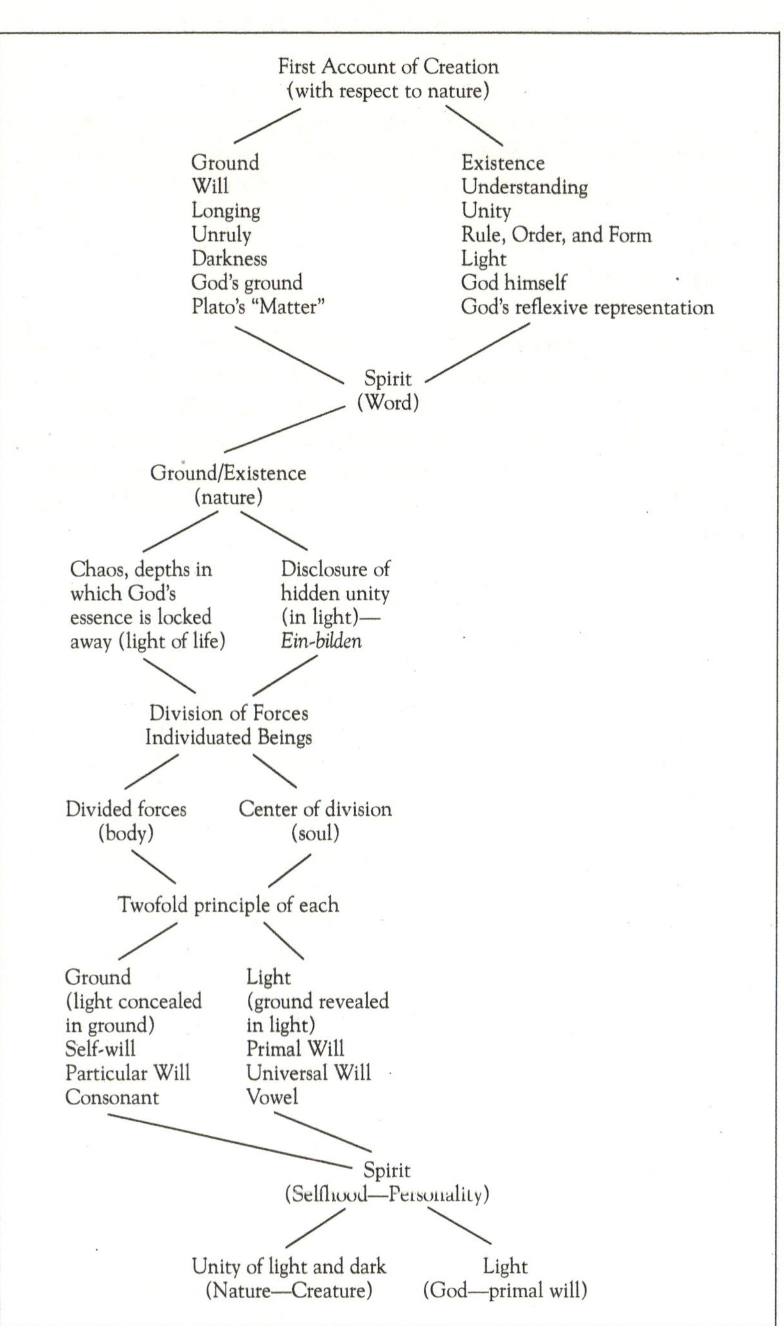

FIGURE 3.1

> though an initial unruliness (*ein anfänglich Regelloses*) had been brought to order. This is the incomprehensible basis of reality in things, the remainder that can never be contained (*der nie aufgehende Rest*), cannot be resolved into reason by the greatest exertion but remains in the depths. Out of that which lacks understanding (*Verstand*), true understanding is born. (359–60)

Although existence and ground are equiprimordial, there is *excess* in the ground that has no counterpart on the side of existence. While Schelling speaks of it in quasimathematical terms, the remainder is not to be thought as something merely "left over" after a process that yields an integral result has been completed. Rather, the unruly is the living genesis of all things, but is not itself a "thing" and can never be exhausted by its animating function.

The unruly–excessive, of course, is not evil. However, it is the necessary condition for the activation of the principles such that evil as well as good become possible. In this sense, the equiprimordial unruly can be regarded as ontologically more significant.

3. Life is the gathering of the unruly and form (rule). Again there is no priority of one over the other. Life is nothing apart from this gathering, and this gathering of the two is nothing apart from life. Separability is always separability in *logos*.

4. To say, however, that separability is always separability in *logos* is far from saying that this separability is *merely* apparent. Rather, the separability—the twoness of the twofold—is required for there to be a showing at all. The account of creation presents the showing of the divine being to himself in a likely account. Thus, this separability accounts for the possibility of anything like *appearing*. With *logos* the very possibility of genesis, of differentiation, and of intelligibility arises. At the same time, *logos* allows for the possibility of destruction, collapse, and chaos. Indeed *logos* both brings forth the two sets of possibilities and depends upon them.

5. Schelling's remarks that directly concern themselves with *logos* in the account are to be understood in this fashion. The key remark involves a remarkable transformation of a crucial passage in the New Testament book of John. After referring to the primal longing as "a surging, billowing sea, similar to the 'matter'[22] in Plato . . . incapable itself of forming anything that can endure" (360) Schelling writes:

> But there is born in God himself an inward reflexive representation corresponding to this longing. . . . This representation is the first in which

> God, viewed absolutely, is actualized, though only in himself; it is in the beginning with God, and the god begotten in God himself. This representation is at the same time understanding the *word* of that longing, and the eternal Spirit, who at once senses the word and the eternal longing, moved by love which he himself is, speaks out the word, such that now understanding becomes freely creating and all-powerful will, and forms nature, which in the beginning was unruly, into its element or tool. (360–61)

Thus, God himself is first of all creative deed, in which *logos* is at once creator in the sense of bringing something forth (namely God himself to himself), and created in the sense of being brought forth (namely God as "self"-created) in the deed of creation. The reinterpretation of John involves a shift that dramatically and radically transforms the understanding of the divine. If one wished to characterize this transformation in Biblical terms, one might say that instead of "*houtos gar egapesen ho theos ton kosmon* (for God so loved the world out of a 'charitable love [*agape*]')," [23] Schelling reads: "*houtos gar eros* (out of an erotic, i.e., a needful love)." But like the separability of God and ground, *agape* of God is one with the *eros* of nature, and the distinction occurs only in *logos*. However, *agape* needs *eros* in order to come forth at all.

6. Bringing the discourse here down to a more earthly level, the birth of God is complete only in humanity.

> For the eternal spirit speaks out the unity or the word in nature. The expressed (real) word, however, is only in the unity of light and darkness (vowel and consonant).[24] To be sure now, there are both principles in all things, but without complete consonance on account of what is lacking in that which has been raised out of the ground. Therefore, only in man is the word, still held back and incomplete in all other things, fully expressed (articulate). But in the expressed word, spirit reveals itself, i.e., God as existing *actu*. Insofar, now, as the soul is the living unity of both principles, it is spirit; and spirit is in God. If, now, in the soul of man the identity of both principles were just as indissoluble as they are in God, there would be no difference, i.e., God as spirit would not be revealed. The same unity that is indivisible in God must therefore be divisible in man, and this is the possibility of good and evil. (363–64)

The seemingly harmless "real" in parentheses immediately following the word[25] "expressed" (*ausgesprochene*) deserves close attention. Reality is fundamentally *expression*, articulation. And since expression is itself the act of creation, expression (articulation) is the gathering of ideal (the principle of light) and real (the principle of darkness).[26] In the act that articulates the word, life shows itself as the simultaneous gathering of ideal and real. No temporal precedence is implied: The eternal act is outside of time. Life did not precede the principles, nor did the principles precede life. The separability of ideal and real is therefore rooted in their fundamental togetherness. That they can be separated "only" in speech, in *logos*, is correct. This "only," however, must not be understood as in any sense privative. For *only* on account of their togetherness in *logos* is their separability possible, and *only* through *logos* can the two be said to come to be at all.

A showing of freedom occurs through the *muthos* of *logos* given in the first account of creation. This showing accounts for all of the distinctions made thus far in the *Freedom Essay*, as well as for the possibility of the *Freedom Essay* itself. *Logos* (as the word) is first made fully articulate in humanity. To say the same thing in another way, primal being as simultaneous first comes fully to show itself in humanity. Yet the showing in man of *logos* occurs successively. What, then, is the human being? The human being *is* this showing of the simultaneous (the eternal act) within the successive (speech within time). This characterization of the human being accounts for Schelling's earlier oracular remark that the philosopher is the one who conceives the god outside with the god within. Thus, the act of *logos* of the philosopher that gathers simultaneous and successive, infinite and finite, part and whole, light and dark, divine and human—this act belongs to *neither* side of these dyads. Rather in the philosophical act, the "members" of these dyads come to be seen together as necessary to and for one another. Here too is the answer to the earlier provocation concerning the possibility of a stance that is neither infinite nor finite: In the human being's act of *logos*, both the infinite and the finite find their place.

How, then, does the philosophical act differ from the eternal act, if it differs at all? Indeed, the accounts above of the two acts are strikingly similar. There is an undeniable sense in which the acts are one, and an undeniable sense in which the acts are two, diverse and distinct. Schelling's word for the way in which creation stands in relation to the divine likewise names the way in which the philosophical act stands to the eternal act: *E i n-b i l d u n g* (362, emphasis in original). The philosophical act *images* the divine act, creatively shaping it into a one.[27] Recalling the discussion of the *Timaeus*, the most appropriate way of speaking of the relation of the divine to the human is not in terms of causality but in terms of *imagination*. The reason for this insistence should now be clear. The relation of the divine to the human, of the simultaneous to the successive, is one of *need*. The divine cannot come to manifestation at all without the human. The human is, in a basic sense, the divine come to life.

Drawing this together now with the central "topic" of the *Freedom Essay*, this showing of the divine in humanity is a showing of the human being to himself. The recognition of this showing occurs by means of a *provocation* that is called a contradiction in logical terms. At this point in Schelling's discourse, it can be reconceived as a conflict (*polemos*). The conflict involves the two principles in their various manifestations. The two principles at war in human beings are in one sense separable, insofar as they show themselves as distinct. In another sense they are inseparable, as the selfsame human being is always the place of the conflict. Insofar as man performs the deed of reflection in which the two principles become manifest as two, and accordingly spirit as selfhood is free of both principles, the showing of the whole to itself in the showing of the philosopher to himself occurs as *human freedom*. Human freedom has its possibility established by the account, insofar as selfhood stands above the two principles. As so standing, it may subordinate either one to the other. In this way, the possibility of evil is shown in the free subordination of the principle of light (universal will) to the principle of darkness (particular will). The deed of bringing this possibility to *logos* was called forth by the feeling of freedom, by the desire (*eros*) to bring freedom to *logos*.

Thus, the distinction between feeling, fact, and concept of freedom mentioned in the first sentence of the work provided the *Freedom Essay*'s first provocation. Though the feeling lay immediately in each, the fact required more than common clarity to be brought to an adequate concept. This concept has just been supplied in the *Freedom Essay*. Standing at the center is the fact of freedom. This fact is announced in the feeling, which in Schelling's words is the "billowing" of the dark principle, like Plato's *hule* (matter) that is without understanding, form and order. Yet this matter has a presentiment of that which it seeks and needs in order to realize itself. But human freedom lies in neither the feeling alone nor the concept alone, nor—unless one speaks very loosely—in the synthesis of these two. Freedom is concretely *fact* as the gathering of the two, and unless the synthesis is seen as not prior to but simultaneous with this gathering, it would be improper to speak of a "placing together."

Thus, to call human freedom the central "topic" is to recollect the Greek sense of *topos*: place, being in place. The human being is the place at which freedom, in showing itself in the way that it does, shows the whole as *living* whole (system in the genuine sense). Immediately given in feeling, yet requiring mediation to be brought to an adequate concept, human freedom is the place where the whole becomes aware of itself as such, or, to speak otherwise, where God gives birth to himself.

But the *Freedom Essay* is charged with more than merely bringing human freedom to a correct concept. The investigations seek the *essence* of human freedom. According to the tradition to which Schelling belongs, *essence* answers the question "*ti estin?* (what is it?)." It is the "*to ti en einai* (what it is, the 'essence')" of the "*ti estin?*" Yet the first account of creation rather peculiarly seems to say nothing with respect to what human freedom distinctively *is.* It concludes with the insight that the possibility of subordinating the universal will (principle of light) to the particular will (principle of darkness) resides in the human being.[28] A further consequence is that when this subordination occurs, the human being uses what exists only *for the sake of* the creature *against* the creature instead. In consequence, the divine measure and balance of the principles is disrupted: This is the nature of evil. The breaking forth of evil shows itself in life, not as life's destruction but rather as its falsification:

> As a true life could only exist in the original relation, there thus arises what is a proper (*eignes*) life, but it is a false life, a life of lies, a growth of disquiet and corruption. The most appropriate likeness is here offered by disease, which, as the disorder that arises through the misuse of freedom in nature, is the true counterimage of evil and sin. (366)

Thus, nothing can be said with respect to the essence of human freedom, and more specifically with respect to the distinctiveness of human freedom, that could not also be said of necessity. The elements of both are identical. They are the elements of the whole as such, and to distinguish human freedom from necessity by means of "the objects connected with it" is impossible. As Schelling points out, it is no ataxia of forces but their false unity that is evil. Over and above these "connected objects," human freedom is nothing at all. Nor is human freedom anything "in addition to" these objects. Nor, at least strictly speaking, is human freedom anything *outside* these objects.

Schelling has called human freedom a power or a faculty (*Vermögen*), the power for good and evil. Thus, properly speaking, freedom is neither good nor evil, although good and evil are each marks of a free act. I strongly suggest that this peculiar state of affairs points to what is indeed distinctive about human freedom: its irreducibility, its opacity. While freedom shows itself in human deeds, it conceals its essence. To say something at least similar if not the same, it belongs to the essence of human freedom to conceal itself. However, human freedom shows itself only in acts that are not sufficient to prove even its possibility. For such a proof (*apodeixis*), another, further account is required that responds to the provocation of human freedom's opacity.

The enigmatic unified/twofold showing of freedom necessitates the way of speaking in the *Freedom Essay*. On one hand, its speaking accounts for the intelligibility of freedom, and therefore may be said to issue from *logos* as reason. On the other hand, the opacity of freedom may be said to issue from *logos* as *muthos*. This twofold speaking occurs with respect to the human being as well. The human being is aware of himself *as* an image, that is, as limited and so requiring thought. The thought required is appropriately spoken of rationally, in terms of proof and deduction. The human being is also an image for which the original is present as *absent*. Thus, the apprehension of the original (God) is spoken of mythically. And, like all else in the *Freedom Essay*, the two "folds" of speaking are nothing apart from their togetherness in life.

The Account of the Actuality of Freedom

> We have sought to derive the concept and the possibility of evil from first principles and to discover the universal fundament of the doctrine that lies in the distinction between existence and that which is the ground of existence. But possibility does not include actuality and the latter is properly the greatest object of the question. (373)

THE POSSIBILITY OF EVIL having been demonstrated in the previous section, Schelling's task in this section is comprised of three parts. The first is to show how evil became actual. Further, it is to explain how it became universally effective. Finally, it is to account for how evil burst forth as an unmistakable feature of creation. However, this task cannot be undertaken directly from the outcome of the previous section. Something more is required, since "possibility does not include actuality." Another Schellingian provocation arises. The way the possibility of freedom was demonstrated cannot be the way the actuality of freedom can be demonstrated, given their difference. Yet the way of demonstration must be the same, in order to preserve the unity of the act of creation. Further, the way of speaking in this new section closely resembles the speaking in its predecessor. So another question presents itself: In what sense does possibility exclude actuality? What more is required for actuality than is required for possibility?

The statement that possibility does not include actuality is especially surprising in light of Kant's *Critique of Pure Reason*, in which the scope of possibility is shown to be no wider than the scope of actuality in the section entitled "The Postulates of Empirical Thought in General." But the Postulates cannot help but gesture toward what they deny.

❧

Again, a careful reading of Kant followed by a glance in the direction of Plato illuminate Schelling's thought in the *Freedom Essay*. Although the section on "Postulates of Empirical Thought" establishes the coextensiveness of possibility and actuality, possibility and actuality (also necessity) for Kant are principles of a thought that must limit itself to what is given through sensibility in order to arrive at objective validity. Thus, the postulates are postulates of *empirical* thought, and therefore possibility and actuality in these postulates apply only to a thought so limited. "The principles of modality [i.e., the Postulates] are therefore nothing but explanations of the concepts of possibility, actuality and necessity in their empirical employment only, and prohibiting their transcendental use" (A219, B266–67). These concepts determine no object, either with regard to its mathematical character or with regard to the rules of time-determination. They merely "express the relation of the concept to our faculty of knowledge" (A219, B266).

The distinction of the possible from the actual in the *Critique of Pure Reason*, then, has nothing to do with the quantity of "objects" connoted by each concept. Possible and actual are not the names of intersecting sets with the former having many more members than the latter. Rather, what distinguishes the actual from the possible is "connection with the material conditions of experience," that is, connection with perception. Not one single mark is added to the object by a judgment of actuality, but merely its relation to the faculty of knowledge. To call the postulates "principles of the pure understanding" that make experience possible is to say that every judgment "A is B" must implicitly be preceded by an "it is possible that . . ." an "it is actual that . . ." or an "it is necessary that . . . ," each of which affirms a different relation of the judgment to the understanding.

Thus, in one sense, more is required for actuality than for possibility: namely, connection with perception. But in another sense, the judgment of something as possible says nothing more about what is in question than a judgment of something as actual (or as necessary): "It does indeed seem as if we were justified in extending the number of possible things beyond that of the actual, on the ground that something must be added to the possible to constitute the actual. But this [alleged] process of adding to the possible I refuse to allow. For that which would have to be added to the possible, over and above the possible, would be impossible" (A231, B284).

If one wished to speak of the realm of the possible extending beyond that of the actual, the only alternative would be to declare that in addition to the series of phenomena that we are given, another kind of entity is somehow present beyond our experience. What can be said about this other kind of entity? In terms of the limits to human knowledge established in the Transcendental Analytic, its possibility can neither be ruled in or ruled out. This possibility, since it would lie beyond the scope of the schematized categories, lacks sense and significance (*Sinn und Bedeutung*). In the Transcendental Dialectic, as we have already seen with respect to freedom, such a realm of phenomena is possible in a different, far looser and more problematical sense than the concept of possibility explained in the postulate: "What is possible only under conditions which themselves are merely possible, is not *in all respects* possible. But such [absolute] possibility of things extends further than experience can reach" (A232, B284). Therefore, the realm of the possible extends no further than the actual. Both are determined by the understanding in its function as making experience possible, in its connection with sensibility (pure intuition).

"In the *mere concept* of a thing no mark of its existence is to be found" (A225, B272). This crucial insight in the section on the postulates accounts at once for the need of "something more" for actuality over against possibility, and for the "nothing more" (A225, B272) in the sense that the actual does not comprise a subset within the possible. The ambiguity of this result is also present in Schelling's thought. It accounts for the similarity of the *logoi* both in this section that considers actuality, and in the previous one that considered mere possibility. However, it is necessary to penetrate still more deeply into the matter of possibility and actuality in the work of Kant in order to gain insight into the way Schelling effects another creative appropriation of his great predecessor.

Schelling gives a clue in one of his earliest works, where he writes in the following footnote: "Perhaps never on so few pages have so many deep thoughts been pressed together as has occurred in Section Seventy-Six of the Critique of Teleological Judgment."[1] In this telling section, Kant discusses the relation of possibility and actuality in terms of human finitude:

> It is indispensably necessary for the human understanding to distinguish between the possibility and the actuality of things. The ground for this lies in the subject and in the nature of our cognitive faculties. Such a distinction (between the possible and the actual) would not be given were there not requisite for knowledge two quite different elements, understanding for concepts and sensible intuition for objects corresponding to them. If our understanding were intuitive, it would have no objects but those which are actual. Concepts (which merely extend to the possibility of an object) would disappear.[2]

Thus, the distinction between the possible and the actual is rooted in the finite character of human knowing. In humans, thought is needed in order to compensate for the fragmentary character of human intuition (A19, B33). Here, thought is the sign of this need, since thought supplies the unity that human intuition lacks. Were there no need, there would be no thought (no concepts), and intuition would not be sensible. That is, our intuition would not be fragmented, would not be given in parts. However, this limited nature of human reason enables Kant to provide "an illustration" of divine knowing that does not at all form "part of the proof" (B72) of his doctrine of intuition. This divine knowing that Kant comes to "illustrate" can now be seen in a different light: In Kant's discussion of possibility and actuality in §76 of the Critique of Teleological Judgment, together with §8, IV of the Transcendental Aesthetic, Kant foreshadows the way of knowing the god outside from the god within. This knowing, nascent in Kant, is brought to fullness by Schelling.

This way is indicated in a seldom-cited section of the Ideal of Pure Reason: "While the idea gives rules, the ideal serves as the archetype (*Urbild*) for the permanent determination of the copy; and we have no other rule of our actions but the conduct of that divine man within us, with which we compare ourselves, and by which we judge and better ourselves, though we can never reach it" (A569, B597). Thus, the self-limiting of the critical philosophy to knowledge of appearances has a twofold positive side. It not only secures the domain in which reason has clearly established rights, it also points to the nature of what lies beyond these secured domains by means of what lies enclosed within them. These two positive senses are clearly akin, and may be properly seen as a silent wellspring out of which Schelling's *Freedom Essay* flows. For, on the one hand, the theme of appropriate limit recurs throughout. On the other hand and simultaneously, the whole as primordial act pervades it.

In this regard, Schelling's statement that possibility does not include actuality serves to draw up the limit of the way of speaking in the *Freedom Essay*. It is a speaking that continually recognizes itself as human. As such, the following qualities belong to it: (1) it is a needful speaking, bound to what is given; (2) the unity it presents is not original; and (3) it is ever cognizant of the ignorance to which it is bound by its nature. In the same way, however, the statement that possibility does not include actuality serves as a sign of the nature of the whole. Insofar as human reason binds thought to intuition out of a need that is in its most fundamental sense erotic (*eros* as primordial unifier), the unification which human reason effects may be seen as a sign of the divine, eternal love that occupies much of the discussion of the actuality of freedom.

Another way of access to Schelling's creative appropriation of the possibility/actuality discourse in the history of philosophy occurs in *Republic* V of Plato, in the sweeping image of their separability and togetherness that animates the discussion of the city in speech. Socrates, Adeimantus, Glaucon, and Thrasymachus address the question to Socrates of whether the city that they have been building in speech is *possible*. Socrates playfully avoids the question:

> Let me take a holiday like the idle men who are accustomed to feast their minds for themselves when they walk along. And such men, you know, before finding out in what way something they desire can exist (*estai*), put the question aside so they won't grow weary deliberating about what's possible or not. They set down as given the existence (*einai*) of what they want and go on to arrange the rest and enjoy giving a full account of the sort of things they'll do when it has come into being. I, too, am by now soft myself. . . . (458a1–b1)

Socrates seems to disjoin the possible from the actual. However, this disjunction does not concern itself with the realization of ideals, as it does in Kant. Rather, the most important division is that of speech from deed, of *logos* from *ergon*. This distinction founds any disjunction between "ideal" and "real."

> Can anything be done as it is said? Or is it the nature of acting to attain to less truth than speaking, even if someone doesn't think so? Do you agree that it is so or not? I do agree. Then don't compel me necessarily to present it as coming into being in every way in deed as we described it in speech. (473a1–3)

Acting (*praxis*) is named as less true than speaking (*lego*). The nature of speech is such that what is said lies beyond the reach of action. The disjunction, therefore, between the possible (set forth in *logos*) and the action indicated by the possible (*praxis*) rests upon the limits of human action in its relation to speech.

However, this relation indicates that *logos* also *calls forth praxis*. The possible calls forth the actual, or at least *can* call forth the actual. Thus, the disjunction is not radical. Socrates responds to the continued challenge of his interlocutors in the following way:

> Then don't compel me to show that what we've described in speech can necessarily come into being entirely as deed (*ergo*). Rather, if we're

> able to discover how a city could come to be ruled in a way that most closely approximates our description, let's say that we've shown what you ordered us to show, namely that it's possible for our city to come to be. (473a5–b1)

It would be incorrect, however, to conclude that reciprocity obtains between them. Gathering the insights of the above paragraphs, (1) the possible and the actual do not stand together, and (2) just as unmistakably, they *do* stand together. The crucial factor is the way these two—the standing together and standing apart of possibility and actuality—are *thought* together. A key phrase that speaks throughout this part of the dialogue is "*me anagkaze* (not by necessity)." The bond of possibility and actuality is not sealed by necessity. The two stand, one might say, in no need of one another. To speak in another idiom, there is no sufficient reason for the gathering of possibility and actuality. No law, no necessity, compels their coming together.

For the sake of the dialogue and in terms of the sweeping movement of the dialogue itself, this phrase accomplishes the disjunction of the necessary from the possible and the actual. With the withdrawal of necessity from the possible and the actual, this bond itself is withdrawn or at least rendered problematic. This withdrawal indeed indicates radical fragmentation. If this fragmentation is seen as occurring in speech, then it follows that *logos*, as articulating the possible and the actual, separates and sunders rather than gathers and unifies. One can read *Republic* I–IX (but not X) as exhibiting *logos* in its power as separator from necessity.

However, to say that "close approximation" in actuality is sufficient to establish possibility is to say that just as the possible calls forth the actual as actual, action (*praxis*) confirms the possible as possible. This distance between them simultaneously establishes the distance and the togetherness of the possible and the actual, of *logos* and *ergon*. The Greek word for "close approximation" is "*eggutata*," literally "as near as possible." Both human possibility and human limit are disclosed in Plato's word "*eggutata*." Again, both separability and inseparability must be thought together.

How, then, can one understand this separation that is both sharply drawn and far from radical? Socrates' remark before beginning his answer gives a very strong hint: The first words in Greek are "*Paradeigmatos ara heneka* (It was therefore for the sake of a paradigm . . .)":

> It was therefore for the sake of a paradigm, I said, that we were seeking both for what justice by itself is like, and for the perfectly just man, if he

should come into being, and what he would be like. . . . We were not seeking them for the sake of proving that it's possible for those things to come into being. (472c4–d2)

Speaking for the sake of a paradigm leaves proof of possibility aside. It, therefore, does not take human nature in its limitedness into account. The pointing out of this omission does not constitute an argument against such speaking for the sake of a pattern. Rather, it serves to show what is said and what is not said in the speaking. Further, in the very deed of speaking "for the sake of a paradigm," another kind of speaking is suggested. This other kind does account for limited and fallible human nature. This latter kind speaks not for the sake of a paradigm but for the sake of humanity. Can both ways somehow join? The answer will be provided in *Republic* X.

Speaking for the sake of the paradigm also bears witness to the separation of possibility from actuality. From this way of speaking, such matters as falling short in "the realization of ideals" whether of cities or of souls becomes understandable, for there is no necessary reason why what is merely possible must become actual. But another kind of speaking treats paradigms, and in a very different manner.

As has been indicated earlier in the discussion of Plato's *Timaeus*, mythical speaking both accounts for the limited nature of humanity and for the kind of access to that which lies beyond what is available to the human being. *Muthos* brings the *paradeigmata* forth *in images*. Thus, *muthos* provides a sighting of the paradigms while paying homage to the bond of speech to imagery, and therewith the bond of man to the earth. The most appropriate speaking regarding paradigms is not, therefore, speaking *for the sake of* the paradigms. Rather, it is a speaking in which the paradigms are brought to images for the sake of humanity. This does not occur in its fullest sense, and does not occur at all with respect to possibility, actuality, and necessity, until the very end of *Republic* X.

In the myth of Er, the paradigms are gathered for the sake of human life. The myth presents a beautiful image of the just life, accounting for its possibility and calling such a life forth into practice. Er's account presents what is absent in the discourse in *Republic* I–IX and expressly excluded from the interplay of possibility and actuality: the rule by Necessity (*Anagke*) of the whole. In the speech for the sake of the paradigm, the necessary is sundered from the possible and the actual, as also it is sundered from the good in another speech a bit later (493b-c). In the myth that gathers up the *Republic* as a whole at the end, the nature of their togetherness is given in an image. The myth does not (indeed cannot) contradict the speech for the sake of the paradigm. Rather, its presentation in a beautiful image shows the connection of the possible and the actual to be fundamentally *erotic* rather than logical, geometrical, or pragmatic. The gathering of the actual to the possible is commanded by a need far stronger ("more stinging [*drimuterai*]" in Glaucon's words at *Republic* 458d6) than any of the latter: *eros*. The mythical speaking itself, by presenting a beautiful image of life (and providing a vicarious image for Glaucon in the context of the dialogue), enacts this erotic necessity. It does so as "seducing" the human being to enact the myth of Er, by choosing wisely.

The myth presents the cycle of life, after death but before rebirth. The spindle of Necessity grants the human being lots from which he can choose a life. This granting images the limitedness of humanity insofar as the lots are finite in number and have already been fashioned. These lots are the paradigms of human lives. A wise choice, made in accord with the practice of philosophy (the pursuit of wisdom), remains possible even to those last in line.[3] Such a choice always involves thoughtful care in the selection of a soul. Foolish choice occurs when the chooser grabs at power, wealth, etc., without studying the entire lot for the delineation of the awful consequences of such a life. The eye of the wise chooser always remains fixed on justice. With respect to the choice of a human life, the possible and the actual stand in no need of one another. The paradigms spoken of by the philosopher may soar above one's lowly human nature and may never be chosen. Yet necessity forces a choice, and grants the possibility of our choosing well.

The *Republic*'s concluding *muthos* gestures beautifully toward our human sojourn on earth. It would be mistaken to read the myth as referring to an accurate account of the netherworld. Rather, the myth stands entirely in service to *this life*. Necessity has made itself manifest by situating us in ways over which we have no control (nation, gender, language, and so on). Yet plenty of room for choice exists within this fate to which we are handed over. This choice is always *our* choice, and is always available. Interpreting the lot chosen before our birth in a (admittedly clumsy) nonmythical manner, if we live an examined life, we ourselves fill out the details merely outlined in the lot.

Looking ahead to the end of the *Freedom Essay*, one glimpses the texture of Schelling's thought in his repetition of an old saying: "This is the secret of love, that it unites such beings as could each exist for itself, and nonetheless neither is, nor can be, without the other" (408). With this in mind, the logical integrity of both the possible and the actual is admitted.

However, this mere logical integrity involves a dead logic, one that must be given life by the "warm breath of love." The mere, abstractly logical is a falsification of the primordially aesthetical. The section on the actuality of evil is charged to unfold this aesthetical dimension.

❧

This explanation of the actuality of evil concerns "not simply how evil came to be real in individual men but its universal effectiveness and how it burst forth from creation as undeniably universal, everywhere battling against the good" (373). The possibility of evil has been shown to be the separability of principles in man, such that the divine measure (harmony) of the principles is disrupted. The creature strives to elevate self-will (particular will) away from its wholesome relation in the center (as given over to universal will), and toward self-centeredness (*hubris*) in which universal will is subjugated to particular will. The section of the actuality of evil is charged to show precisely how this separation comes about. In terms of the *muthos* of the *Freedom Essay*, this question is the same as the question of the actuality of the self-revelation of God. The separability of principles is necessary for God's self-revelation, since without this separability there would be no distinction of creatures from God. If there is no distinction of creatures from God, there is neither birth nor revelation. Thus, the birth of God requires something more than the possibility in speech of separation. The principles must actually be separated in order for God to reveal himself. That is to say, in order to reveal himself God must undergo evil. But in order to be God, he must be unstained by it. Yet if God did not reveal himself, God would not live and so would not be God. The section on the actuality of evil is animated by the reflection that God, in undergoing the separability of principles, risks himself in coming to life—indeed *must* risk himself. There is a need in God to undergo evil of which he is not the cause.

The root of the separation of the principles in humanity is neither the self-will of the human being as creature nor in the universal will. Rather, the basis of the separation cannot be said to lie in the will at all but is antecedent to all will. Schelling writes:

> The human being has been placed on that summit where he contains within him the source of self-impulsion towards good and evil in equal measure; the nexus of principles in him is not a bond of necessity but of freedom. He stands at the dividing line; whatever he chooses will be his

> act, but he can not remain in indecision because God must necessarily reveal himself and because nothing at all in creation can remain ambiguous. Nonetheless it seems as though he could not escape indecision, just because it is indecision. (374)

Schelling's name for that which calls forth the decision of man in which God's self-revelation occurs is "solicitation." The solicitation is a temptation to evil, which appears seductive and desirable. The solicitation is antecedent to the will with its bond to freedom (with respect to the principles) in the sense that only by virtue of the solicitation does the will come forth *as will* for the human being. That is, in order to become aware of the twofoldness of the principles and the very bond of freedom, an enticement that sets the twofoldness of principles at odds must occur. *Love* connotes the harmony of the principles. The enticement of evil occurs in order to call this harmony to life by the provocation of its absence in discord. This provocation calls attention to the possible concord of the principles, and so to the divine love. In this way the solicitation to evil allows for the revelation of the divine love. This love is revealed in humanity alone. But the divine love had to risk itself in order for its revelation. It had to risk its falsification as lust and gratification of base desires, and as the desire for mastery that also calls itself love. That is, in order to reveal himself, God had to undergo the risk of human freedom. The solicitation to evil begets the risk.

Thus, the account of the actuality of evil is the account of a God in need. This account belongs intimately to the disclosure of the essence of human freedom. Whereas the account of the possibility of evil was simultaneously the account of creation with respect to nature, the account of actuality is an account of creation with respect to *history*, that is, an account of the occurrence of evil in time according to first principles. And whereas the former account culminates in the human being as the making-fully-articulate of the principles, the latter account culminates in the human being who, having undergone evil in human history, affirms the free unity of the principle (their harmony) as ordained by a divine necessity. That is, just as the account of creation according to nature reaches its highest expression in man as creature, the account according to history reaches its highest expression in man as spirit. The image in which these "two highest points" are joined is "the exemplary and divine man, he who in the beginning was with God, and in whom all other things and man himself were created"[4] (377).

The following chart is designed to present the actuality of evil as the account of creation according to history. "The birth of spirit is the realm of

Second Account of Creation
(with respect to History)
Ground
Will
Longing
Unruly
Darkness
God's ground
Plato's "Matter"
Existence
Understanding
Unity
Rule, Order, and Form
Light
God himself
God's reflexive representation
Spirit
(Word)
Existence/Ground
(History)
(Second) principle
of light (selfhood
subordinated to light)
(Second) principle
of darkness (selfhood
elevated above light)
Division of Wills
(Good and Evil Men)
Spirit of love
(Unity—dark
subordinated
to light)
Spirit of evil
(Disunion—light
subordinated
to dark)
Twofold principle in each Human
Universal Will
(Primal basis
revealed in light
through bond of love)
Particular Will
(Primal basis
striving for
self-actualization)
Spirit
(fully actualized selfhood—personality)
Nature
History
(Unity of striving basis
and will to light)

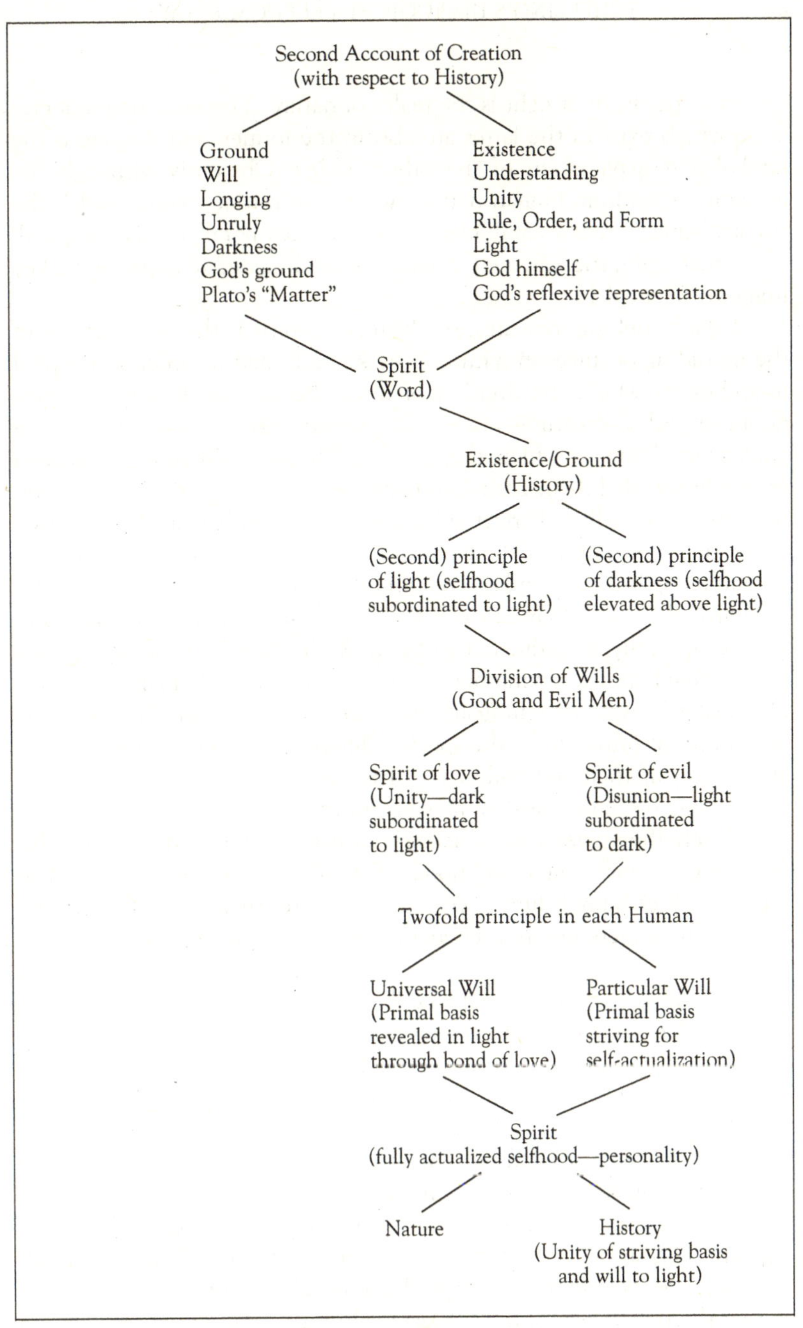

FIGURE 4.1

history as the birth of light is the realm of nature. The same stages of creation which exist in the latter are also in the former, and the one is the symbol and explanation of the other" (378). Obviously, although the account begins from human nature (where the initial account ends), the two accounts present a simultaneous event. No temporal priority is implied.

Once again, the following comments are designed to animate the key items on Figure 4.1:

1. As Schelling indicates, the history of spirit is the mirror image of the unfolding of stages in nature. Just as nature had to occur as a graded unfolding in which the division of forces became gradually more pronounced and so creatures more individuated, history had to occur as a graded unfolding in which the forces of divine spirituality (goodness) gradually revealed themselves in humanity so as to reach final completion in perfect spirituality. Perfect spirituality occurs in a man distinguished from other men solely by the bond of the divine love within him. As the human being is the exemplary creature, the only one in whom the word is fully articulate, the divine man is the exemplary man, the one in whom the word is fully subordinated to light. With respect to the question of human freedom, the divine man is the one in whom human freedom is identical with what Schelling later will call a holy necessity. Insofar as the divisibility of principles is the specific difference of human freedom, the affirmation of their indivisibility in the divine man serves as an image toward which human freedom may be drawn.

2. Schelling gives a likely account of history in accordance with this unfolding of spirit out of selfhood (378–80). In this account, God as nature realizes himself fully according to nature; then, upon the dissolution to which mere nature is fated, God enters as spirit giving

> a new division of peoples and tongues, a new realm in which the living word enters as a firm and enduring center in battle against chaos, and a declared state of war between good and evil commences . . . in which God reveals himself as spirit, i.e., as real actuality. (380)

It would seem, therefore, that the Greeks are seen as symbols of a word not yet fully personal for Schelling, although the Greek experience of the divine is no less genuine and the whole is no less present. But perhaps this falls short of Schelling's view. Perhaps, that is, the task of unfolding history as succession within simultaneity calls not only for an accounting for the polytheism of the Greeks in their time but also a recollection of the Greeks as eternally present, as the *depth* of the one moment.[5]

3. Just as in the unfolding of nature where gradual differentiation of creatures occurred, in the unfolding of spirit in time the ever-gradual further differentiation of spiritual principles occurs, yielding more and more actuality. A consequence most significant for the understanding of the *Freedom Essay* is this: In order for the good to show itself to its highest degree, evil must do likewise. The greatest good must arise out of the greatest evil, ". . . if there were no conflict then love could not become real" (374). "Therefore the will of the basis excites the self-will of the creature . . . so that when the spirit then arises as the will of love it may find an opponent in which it can realize itself" (375–76). The actuality of good demands the actuality of evil. And since in humanity alone God is revealed, the human being must undergo the solicitation of evil in himself in order to realize the good he has been granted.

To use Schelling's words, the human being must undergo the terror of life that drives him out of the center. Only then can the bond of freedom, which shows itself as a holy necessity in the divine man, show itself as (1) a necessity to which human beings are bound, and (2) as a natural necessity that determines other creatures. A sense for the full significance of human freedom as *power* for good and evil emerges here: Power (*Vermögen*) means "potentiality" to be sure, but it also translates as *dunamis* in Plato's *Republic*. In humanity there is the power for the most exalted good, and the power for the most despicable evil.

The view that possibility does not include actuality has still further import. The whole of the divine being is contained in the ground, but *without unity*. The ground—also called the depths, the dark principle, and "Plato's matter"[6]—is pure potentiality in which all possibilities are included, but in which nothing whatsoever *is*.[7] Something else is required of the pure potentiality to give rise to being. This is the principle of light, which is not included in the principle of darkness but is bound to it by the necessity of love. Love needs the dark principle in order to become actual. Thus, good has to undergo evil, light darkness, union discord, and love hatred.

Recollecting the path of the *Freedom Essay*, the account of the dark principle both images and accounts for the power for good and evil in humanity. The account of creation may be seen as an image of human freedom. Human freedom is nothing in the way of an attribute, nothing but a potentiality that itself requires an external provocation (solicitation) in order to awaken at all. Human freedom awakens nothing other than the twofoldness of principles that already dwell in the human being, nothing else. Just as the ground is neither good nor evil, the free human being is neither good nor evil as well.[8] The human being stands in for the ground as the site of God's self-revelation, the revelation of spirit in nature. Thus, man's actuality does not rest upon his freedom but upon his deed, which is nothing other than his freedom (as potential) made actual. Thus, although the human being must pass through evil, must undergo evil and ultimately death, Schelling can say: "Notwithstanding this general necessity, evil ever remains man's own choice; the basis cannot cause evil as such, and every creature falls through his own guilt" (381–82).

The section on the actuality of evil shows how the universal effectiveness of evil arises from the necessity of evil for the birth of the whole. Evil must show itself in a vicarious image (solicitation) to the human being in order to awaken the twofoldness of the principles. Only so is the human being brought to *life* as the struggle of the principles. Given the requirement of a seductive image for the awakening of the principles, the original encounter with the whole is *aesthetic*. Whether considered the unity of the principles in God or in their separability in human beings, the *hen panta* is an erotic unity, and the risk of the whole is the risk that love undergoes in order to become actual.

The birth of God, in which the principle of light (the higher principle) enters the world, must occur as the birth of time. The whole, in order to be what it already is, must undergo the possibility of the most radical fragmentation. It must undergo the possibility of a radical passing away for the sake of the most lively coming to be. That is to say, humanity is the meeting place of being and nonbeing. The fate of the whole rests upon the nothingness of human freedom, or more precisely upon what we can now only call its original neutrality with respect to good and evil.

This does not affirm any parallel between good/evil, on the one hand, and being/nonbeing, on the other hand, for Schelling, who at every turn unmistakably differentiates his thought from scholasticism. Rather, it merely says that the fate of humanity has fallen to humanity. Thus, all opposition and struggle, and therewith all harmony and reconciliation, takes place in humanity. This struggle and this reconciliation must be seen as a vicarious image that the human being, consulting the god within, is called to draw up for himself.

V

The Real Concept of Freedom— The Formal Side

THE NEXT INVESTIGATION concerns the real concept of freedom with respect to its formal side. It presents the intelligibility of the concept of freedom with respect to its place within "a systematic world view." In the first sentence of the *Freedom Essay*, Schelling intimated that the right concept lay deeper beneath the surface than might be surmised. He also claimed that for the concept of freedom to have any reality at all, it must be "one of the dominant central points of the system" (336). The groundwork required for the presentation of the real concept of freedom with respect to its intelligibility has been completed only now, after both accounts of creation have been developed and their unity shown.

This section appears to be a traditional presentation of arguments in which previous views are criticized and the author's own view propounded. However, it provides much more. It gathers up and responds to those provocations in the very first sentence of the *Freedom Essay* concerning the unity of fact, concept, and feeling. In so doing, it connects these provocations with the way the whole makes itself manifest in humanity and in each human being. After exhibiting this connection, the deeper investigation into the essence of human freedom can take place. This deeper investigation points beyond seriousness, struggle, and victory. It transforms and enhances the sense of the whole thus far presented. In addition, it points beyond the philosophy called German Idealism.

Schelling writes: "The intelligible essence of each thing, and especially of each human being, is, as a result of [idealism's raising freedom into the appropriate realm], outside of all causal connections as it is outside or beyond all time" (383). Intelligibility belongs to the realm of understanding, the side (Figure 4.1) of unity, of God himself. The realm is outside all time, "before" all time by its very nature. The formal side of the real concept of freedom concerns its nontemporal, eternal character. Thus, when Schelling says that an insight into this formal side involves no less difficulty than the explanation of its real concept, this means that the intelligibility of freedom rests upon the understanding of the eternal act together with the birth of history, that is, of time. The "method" recurs by which the god outside is discerned from the god within. At this point in the *Freedom Essay*, it finds its locus in the eternal character of freedom in the human being, who discerns this character from his own actions in time. Since speaking of the formal side of freedom issues from within the limits of human apprehension, this speaking is *mythical*.[1]

Schelling discusses the feeling announcing the eternal character of human freedom in the midst of remarks on the immediate relation of the formal sense of freedom to humanity:

> Through it (the act of creation) the human being's life extends to the beginning of creation, since by means of it he is also more than creature, free and himself eternal beginning. Although this idea may seem ungraspable to the common way of thought, there is, however, a feeling in accord with it, as if each man has been what he is from all eternity, and in no sense first came to be in time. (386)

The unfolding of the formal side of freedom is the bringing to *logos* of the feeling. The exhibition of the intelligible ground of the feeling brings the concept to clarity, just as the feeling is the dark ground in which the intelligible concept must realize itself. The feeling serves as the clue to the intelligible ground, and the intelligible ground serves to make the feeling *this* feeling and no other. The arguments concerning the formal side of freedom all issue from the relation between the feeling and the concept (intelligibility) of freedom.

The voluntarist argument (382–83) preserves the integrity of the feeling (as well as the indecision implied in it) without taking account of the independence of time toward which the feeling points. The consequence of this failure is the positing of accidentality, which contradicts the unity of the whole. The Idealist argument accounts for the independence of time but (at least in Fichte) misunderstands evil as free and therefore eternal, and reverts to "humanitarianism," in which evil is seen to be a feature of the inertia of human nature.

The task requires grasping the unity of the eternal and the temporal. It may be called the simultaneity of simultaneity and succession. Freedom must be grasped as wholly and always independent of time, and yet always determinate and manifest in an act. Yet the act appears, occurs, in time. The twofoldness of the character of act as simultaneously free and determined belongs to what Schelling calls the "inner essence" or "the essence of the essence" of humanity. This means that the human being is his own essence. With respect to his humanity, the human being creates himself. This is what Fichte's self-positing says at bottom,[2] and this is what Schelling is driving at with this startling remark:

> The saying *determinatio est negatio* does not in any way apply to this sort of determination, since this is itself one with the position and concept of this essence, thus really being the essence of the essence. The intelligible being, therefore, insofar as it acts absolutely and with full freedom, can as certainly only act according to its own inner nature. Or the activity can follow from its inner nature only in accord with the law of identity, and with absolute necessity that is also the only absolute freedom. (384)

The essence is precisely this absolute action. "The human being's essence is essentially *his own deed*" (385). In other words, although the human being appears in time, he is most fundamentally a simultaneous whole. The essence of the essence, the essence of man as rational animal, is the simultaneous and always self-same deed of man. *Omnis determinatio est negatio* presupposes absolute position, a determination before all determination, and therefore expresses the character of determination only in a relative sense. Instead, in this formulation Schelling has presented a Spinozism free of abstractness: Realism and Idealism are brought together as the self-showing of life. This section presents the need of Spinozism for Idealism and of Idealism for Spinozism:

> If this (inner) essence were a dead being and with respect to man something merely given, it would be the case that acts could only follow from him out of necessity, with all ascribability and freedom cancelled. But this inner necessity is itself freedom. . . . (385)

Thus, life as the gathering of ideal and real produced by their mutual erotic need serves as the way the inner essence is released from the Spinozist bonds of the necessity of nature. Free will, excluded from the deterministic Spinozist system, brings into being and pervades the whole of

Schelling's system. Apart from life there is no freedom. This means that the intelligibility of freedom, its formal side, can only be understood from its immersion and interpenetration in life. Bringing this intelligibility to *logos* requires more than the arguments of Idealism can provide. Indeed, it requires more than any argument can provide.[3]

To say, as Schelling does, that all action according to the inner essence of man follows out of the law of identity is to say that the human being is his own deed. As has been shown, the law of identity is originally creative, bringing forth unity and uniting the two highest laws of all thinking, the laws of identity and of sufficient reason. This creative deed is exhibited in its immediate relation to human freedom and in its essential togetherness with necessity. Insofar as the human being is free and stands outside time, he gives himself his own law. Insofar as this law is made manifest in deeds, his actions follow necessarily according to the principle of sufficient reason, the intelligible law that rules appearances in time (natural necessity). This is the specific difference of human freedom for which Idealism itself could not account: The human being alone is free in the very way he is determined, and that each human being by his own deed beyond all time determines himself eternally. Freedom and fate are identical. To say that the human being is his own deed (is absolute position, is his own eternal act) is to say the human being is compelled to accept what occurs as his own choice. I am compelled to make fate *my* fate.

God alone has the ground of existence in himself. This is why Schelling distinguishes the human act from the primal act. But insofar as the human being is in God, it falls to man to take over this ground by his own act. Again, the acts are simultaneous. The successive character of human action, including the successive character of representation in philosophical investigations, images the eternal, simultaneous deed in which all things perpetually come forth. The corporealization of man (387), which allows and compels his acts to occur in time according to the law of sufficient reason, belongs to the primal act according to the law of identity in which all things burst forth in one, and simultaneously, as *will*.

Thus, the necessity of human action is distinguished from predestination as understood by the scholastics. In scholasticism, predestination consisted of election prior to the being of humanity. Despite any effort on the part of the individual human being, some men and women would lead virtuous lives and others would lead wicked ones. But the human being is nothing other than his own deed, nothing other than act. The only way to understand predestination is that the human being destines himself eternally by his own act. There is no election, nor is there any elector.

Schelling presents the act as *being* (primal being as the eternal act of man's will) and not becoming. This inverts the scholastic understanding in which being is the end in its fullness, and the act of humanity is seen as a coming to be toward the end already contained in being.

In other words, the human being *chooses his fate* in an act that occurs nontemporally. One can therefore speak of "predestination" here only if the "pre" does not refer to a temporal "before" but to a choice made independently from the temporal order. This choice, however, necessarily determines all that will occur for the human being *in* the temporal order. Further, for Schelling, this means that the temporal order is coextensive with the aforementioned atemporal choice. Hence, the becoming of the human being is *not* already contained *de facto* in the divine being. As Schelling wrote, God could take no pleasure in an unfree being, that is, a being unlike himself. This choice, which we have all necessarily made and which achieves ever-ongoing but always partial disclosure, accounts for the possibility of evil in yet another manner.

The formal side of freedom is, therefore, bound up with necessity. It is indeed the same with it. Schelling's remark on predestination affirms this sameness in principle (however much his may differ from the scholastic conception) and exhibits it. But just as the formal sense of freedom requires insight into its connection with the whole, the same requirement applies to necessity. The concept of necessity as rigid determinism, that is, as the counter-concept to freedom, is merely formal. The formal concept can be understood only if it is abstracted from the living whole.

At this point in the *Freedom Essay*, the earlier contention that every nobler ambition of the spirit dies if it is not animated by the contradiction of freedom and necessity (338) becomes intelligible. The meeting of freedom and necessity, their struggle and their reconciliation, characterizes life. Without the contradiction, there can be no life. When this agonistic contradiction ceases to struggle, the death of the human spirit ensues.

The eternal togetherness of freedom and necessity accounts for the way of speaking in this section and reflects back upon the *Freedom Essay* thus far. For here, the contradiction of freedom and necessity is firmly established as a creatively agonistic sameness. The formal concept of freedom returns to its home in the original act. This return is presented mythically, as occurring before the act. Similarly the formal concept of necessity recollects the pull of the ground "before" the act in which existence and ground come together in life. Thus, this presentation of formal freedom and of formal necessity falsifies their co-presence in life. They are pale images that depend for their very possibility upon erotic necessity.

Erotic necessity means *groundless* necessity, necessity prior to any sufficient reason. Freedom and necessity draw together out of a need that is nothing prior to the drawing together. Rather, this need occurs spontaneously and cannot be located nor said to come into being at any time. Just as the drawing together of male and female happens of itself, the coming together of freedom and necessity must be seen as entirely unprovoked, yet as originally provocative.

Thus, speaking of origin is itself a manifestation of the act in which the human being creates himself. With respect to humanity and to individual human beings, freedom hearkens to an act before all time. In this act, the human deed is the act of freedom in which necessity is affirmed. This free act discloses the necessity of humanity to give itself rule, form, and order. Further, this disclosure seals the act as erotic act, called forth by human need and incompleteness. Schelling gives a suggestive hint in this direction when he writes: "In original creation, as has been shown, man is an undecided essence (which may be presented mythically as a condition prior to this life of innocence and original bliss) . . ." (385). This remark not only connects with the mythical status of his account of history in the previous section but illuminates the way of speaking of the *Freedom Essay* in general. The twofoldness of ground and existence, out of which the contradiction of freedom and necessity emerged, is a likely account. As such, the need of the human being to complete himself with respect to self-knowledge is balanced with the human bond to self-ignorance and the (here moral) need to remain within its limits. This is the most fundamental sense in which the human being, though not originally creative, creates himself.

Given our *muthologia*, self-creation is best seen through the analogy of the fashioning of a work of art than through any other. In the account of history, Schelling claims that the instinct of self-preservation is itself the creative factor (376). Instinct and creativity are likewise bound. The philosophical act consists in fashioning an image suitable for human self-preservation. In the latter terms, *human* receives the emphasis. As we have seen, the act is hardly arbitrary but ruled by a necessary law that has been called the law of identity in the creative sense. So understood, this law is coextensive with that oracle according to which the philosopher is the one who knows the god outside from the god within. Therefore, the *Freedom Essay* can be seen as a fateful meeting of modern and Greek thought. To encapsulate this meeting, Kant's insight regarding the sighting of the divine by finite human knowing (especially in §76 of the *Critique of Judgment*) is brought to the beautiful imagery that animates the writings of Plato, especially in the myth of Er.

Schelling distinguishes the image of man developed in the *Freedom Essay* on several occasions from what he calls *philanthropism*, love of humanity. For Schelling, philanthropism is in principle false, since love comes to life in humanity alone. In addition, philanthropism comes too late, missing the original human deed in which the human being chooses himself as good or evil. Further and perhaps most dangerously, philanthropism tacitly finds human needfulness lamentable, requiring indulgence. But immediately after this somewhat unsympathetic discussion, Schelling takes human need into account. He answers an anticipated objection that his view rules out all conversion from evil to good and vice versa. The objection would claim that his account makes the influence of human or divine intervention impossible, and therefore denies efficacy to human deeds:

> However if it happens that human or divine aid—(for some aid man always needs)—determines him to the transformation from evil to good, this nevertheless lies in the fact that he accepts the positive influence of the good spirit, and does not positively exclude it; in any case this is already found in that initiating (*anfänglichen*) act through which he is this man and no other. (389)

Thus, the need of humanity, which is *perpetual* as indicated by the parenthetical remark in the above passage, is rather one with the initiating act. This act brings forth both the birth of god and of the humanity in our creaturely nature. Therefore, the act deserves celebration. In it, the human being chooses his own fate. Finitude gives no excuse for evil. Lamentation insults both God and humanity. The reduction of the initiating act to "human nature" leads to a denial of freedom. Ironically, philanthropy leads to the devaluation of humanity.

The question of a change from good to evil or vice versa, therefore, is meaningless if the eternal character of man's act is left out of account. While all change implies time and becoming, the eternal act in which each human being chooses his life occurs outside of time. And if the eternal character is accounted for, the changes that occur in time are the consequence of the eternal act in which the ordering of the principles occurs in each. The unfolding of each human being's life in time is simultaneously the bringing forth to himself of his own eternal deed. It is meaningless to speak of this deed as temporally prior. The life of humanity in time is nothing other than the fashioning of his own deed, the choosing of his own fate.

In the myth of Er that closes Plato's *Republic*, this unfolding takes place in the choosing of lots. The "place" of this choice is Hades, the realm of the dead disembodied souls, whose task is to choose their next life on earth. This "place" is no place, in no time. The lots determine both the outline and the details of a particular life. Thus, they should be chosen with great care, with thorough study informed by philosophy. Even the last soul "in line" can choose a good life. But "the one who has the first lot will be the first to choose (*haireistho*) a life to which he is bound by necessity (*anagkes*)" (617e2–3). Schelling incorporates and transforms Platonic imagery into a mythical language appropriate to a modern philosophy that nourishes the roots from which it grew. The choice of lots in the myth of Er becomes the ordering of principles in Schelling's *Freedom Essay*:

> In the strictest sense it is true that, however the human being is constituted, it is not he himself but the good or the evil principle that acts in him; and nevertheless this does no violence to freedom. Because precisely the letting-act-in-himself of the good or the evil principle is the consequence of the intelligible deed through which his essence and life is determined. (389)

That the human being must choose either good or evil is not his choice. To choose good or evil, however, is his essence. To say that the letting-act-in-him of either principle determines his life is precisely to say that the intelligible deed draws the striving ground toward itself, making the human being who he is. Since in humanity the whole first becomes a living whole, the choice of each human being must be measured as the choice for all. (This is another instance of Schelling's creative transformation of Kant's moral philosophy.) Thus, the discussion shows that the formal concept of freedom can never be merely formal. It shows the formal side in its active character, that is, as *giving form*—to the one and to the all simultaneously.

The fact of freedom has shown itself as each human being's fatedness to live out his own choice. This fact gathers freedom's concept and its feeling. The gathering occurs according to the law of one's own essence and of the feeling in each human being of his eternal nature. Recalling the first sentence of the *Freedom Essay*, the fact does not lie so near the surface. Bringing the fact to *logos* requires more than common clarity, as the fact is buried in the depths (the ground, the basis). It can be brought to light only by means of reaching into the depths and sighting the heights (the concept of freedom) that draw the depths up into selfhood. In a word, the showing of the essence of human freedom requires *philosophy*.

The Description of the Manifestation of Evil in Humanity

THE DESCRIPTION OF EVIL in humanity exhibits the way the whole is manifest in the human being. That is, the description of evil presents the human being as a sign of the whole. The unity of the god within and the god outside is manifest in the philosophical act of freedom. In this short section, the *Freedom Essay* circles back upon itself. The progress of interpretation in the *Freedom Essay* displays the unfolding of the god outside from the god within. This unfolding issues from human freedom as the possibility of evil (the co-presence of the two principles). The disclosure of human freedom is nothing other than the disclosure of the twofoldness of principles that animate the whole. Thus the whole is brought forth (God is born): The God outside unfolds from the God within, and vice versa. At this point, an earlier and then puzzling remark becomes clearer. Schelling had claimed (358) that in the circle from which all things come into being, it is no contradiction to say that that which gives birth to the one is, in its turn, produced by it.

This circling recalls Socrates' Diotima speech on *eros* in the *Symposium*. This speech presents the birth of *Eros* from father *Poros* (Resource) and mother *Penia* (Poverty) at the divine banquet. The speech performs several functions simultaneously. It speaks about its subject matter appropriately, that is, mythically. It brings *Eros* to birth in *logos*, and brings together material from the previous speeches. In so doing, it circles back to the beginning, when the symposiasts first set the task of bringing *Eros* to birth in *logos*. Schelling's mythical account of the being-in-God of humanity and the being-in-man of God similarly brings freedom to speech and completes the task of showing its centrality. As the speech of Socrates is born of *eros*, so the speech of Schelling is an act of freedom.

The act of philosophical investigation is both interpretation and sign of God's self-revelation, for which real evil is necessary. In terms of the structure of the *Freedom Essay*, this section might be called "the necessity of freedom." For in this section the possibility and actuality of evil are shown to issue from the necessity of evil for the self-revelation of God in humanity. The necessity of freedom as the power for good and evil in humanity makes itself manifest in this showing.

The manifestation of evil can be described only in terms of the bond of the two principles. Evil consists in humanity's elevation of the dark basis of his selfhood to the place where the universal will should be. The spiritual becomes a mere means thereby. The bond of the two principles, then, is not love but strife. The being that is "the reverse of God" rules. This so called "being," properly regarded as a falsification of being, cannot be grasped by "complete understanding." Complete understanding is ruled by light. But in "the reverse of God," the principle of light is subordinated to darkness. Light cannot be seen in its clarity. Schelling calls the falsification of complete understanding "false imagination (*falsche Imagination—logismo notho*)" (390). False imagination: complete understanding::reverse of God (falsification of being): God. The "faculties" are in themselves the same, and are distinguishable only by virtue of the difference of the bond between the principles. Interestingly, Schelling recollects the *Timaeus* in this discussion, likening sin to the grasp of the receptacle in Plato, which occurs through *logismo notho*—through "a bastard, or misbegotten *logos* which is precisely (*eben*) what sin is" (390).

Here one must wonder at Schelling's reading of *logismo notho* as *falsche Imagination* and as sin. In the *Timaeus*, speaking of the dark principle in a "bastard *logos*" was surely said to be difficult and obscure (49a2), but *never* false. Nor does the *khora* represent anything remotely like "evil," or like "sin." Still further, Schelling's own discourse incoporates at least some of the textures of the speaking he has called *logismo notho*. Toward the end of this section, I will address this apparent difficulty in Schelling's thought.

At this point in the text, Schelling's modern description of evil in the human being joins imagery from the *New Testament* and from Plato's *Timaeus*. Since this provides a particularly promising occasion to consider the *Freedom Essay*'s unique dialogue, I shall digress briefly before returning to the matter of the manifestation of evil in humanity.

❧

After speaking of the nature of *nous*, which is always the same, uncreated and indestructible—and right opinion, to which coming to be and passing away (time), belongs—Timaeus mentions a third *genos*, eternal (*aei*), giving a home to all created things, is place (*topos*), which is apprehended by a kind of *logismo notho* (52b2), which leads us to say that necessarily all being is in some place and has a space. By a bastard *logos* then, we affirm (1) a "being" like *nous* insofar as it is eternal and unchanging, and (2) a "being" like becoming (*genesis*) in that we are compelled in order to account for what appears in time. Yet we cannot affirm such a being, since it is nothing at all in itself, apart from *eidos*-giving *nous*. To bring it to *logos* at all is to give it "shape" that it lacks by its nature. It receives this "shape" only through its service as the site of begetting.

Thus, speaking of it apart from begetting is *misbegotten*, a bastard *logos*. And yet, the bastard *logos* is called forth by necessity of being to occur in time. In Schelling, the necessity is erotic. The *Timaeus* presents it in the erotic image of procreation. Generation (becoming) is seen as the child of *nous* (father) and *hupodoxe* (receptacle, mother). Therefore, generation (i.e., appearance, manifestation, revelation) requires *two* equally eternal beginnings (*nous* and *hupodoxe*): (1) pure being, and (2) equally eternal nonbeing as-pure-potential-being. One can see a likeness within their difference: Insofar as *nous* needs a second principle in which to generate itself, it is also potential—potential becoming.

This second equally eternal beginning is the depth of the second realm of history. The scholastic interpretation of Christianity acknowledges this depth. But the difference in its treatment from that in the *Freedom Essay* serves to make Schelling's treatment all the clearer and more radical. For example, Aquinas says of prime matter that because of its pure potentiality it is "far removed from likeness to God." Nevertheless, insofar as it has being in that diminished sense, it retains "a certain likeness to the divine existence."[1] Further, ". . . there is an idea of matter in God, but not distinct from the Idea of the composite of matter and form. For matter in itself neither exists nor can it be known"[2] (a most remarkable statement). These remarks intimate a peculiar twofoldness in which the manner of speaking to prime matter is seriously called into question.[3] However, twofoldness is never interpreted as need in any sense. It is never taken as necessary for the life of God, which is conceived as mere (albeit perfect) self-movement.

Schelling's recollection of the *Timaeus* brings forth the dimension of God's need to give birth to himself. Adding this need to the divine love as free beneficence (*agape*), the divine is seen in a vicarious image. In this image, the human being can see himself both in the pain of birth and in the freedom peculiar to his nature. To be sure, the second beginning of history (presented by Schelling as the advent of Christianity) is the manifestation of a new era. In the *University Studies*, this new era is said to reverse Greek revelation. The Greek gods were those images in which the infinite was perceived in the finite. In the Christian manifestation of the divine, in man the finite is perceived in the infinite. The Greek gods are nature seen as infinite. The divine men of Christianity are the infinite seen as finite. A bond of unity seals the two, both despite and because of this difference. The unities of nature and of history are themselves joined in the unity of *appearing*.

For any appearing, a twofold is required. The recollection of the *logismo notho* in the *Timaeus* is a very striking reminder of this need. In terms of Schelling's theological imagery, there is need for Christianity to recollect its need for "paganism" and its bond to it. In nontheological terms, the meeting of modern and Greek first occurs as an ascent beyond Greek mythological thinking and asserts the rule of reason (Kant). It then circles back to its origin, reaching both its highest and deepest point when it (consciously or not) recollects and incorporates the spirit that gives rise to Greek mythology—and hence itself becomes mythological.

Evil occurs in human beings when the bond of the principles is the reverse of their loving bond. Nevertheless, the bond of the principles in evil is an *imitation* of love. It is a false unity and the falsification of love. In this falsification, what is properly subordinate (selfhood) comes to rule. Schelling discusses evil (sin) as *logismo notho*, understood here as falsification of *logos*, that which would pass itself off as *logos* but is not. He accounts for its occurrence in terms of the difference of humanity from divinity.

> In this, [the enemy of creation] is supported by man's own evil inclinations, for his eye, unable to hold its glance firmly upon the gleam of the divine and the truth, always looks into non-being. So the beginning of sin consists in that man steps over from genuine being to non-being, from truth into falsehood, from light to darkness, in order to become the creative ground himself, and to rule, with the power of the center which he has, over all things. (390)

Thus, evil is not privation of good in terms of lack of perfection (wholeness) as Augustine and the Scholastics maintained. The whole is present in evil in a terrifying manifestation. In evil, the whole is seen as self-consuming and as misshapen and ugly, a perverse amusement-park mirror image of itself as it is in truth. "Manifest sin, unlike mere weakness or impotence, does not fill us with pity but with fear and horror" (391).

The evil in humanity contains a self-destructive principle even as it strives to assert itself as the center and as creative. Nevertheless, evil must speak the word it would strive to break. In terms of Greek imagery, this self-elevation occurs as *hubris* that calls forth *Nemesis*. In terms of modern Kantian thought, this self-elevation occurs as the formation of non-universalizable maxims that ultimately contradict or cancel themselves. In Schelling's language, ". . . Even sin had to become revealed, because only in opposition to sin does the innermost bond of dependence of all things and the essence of God reveal itself, which is b e f o r e (*v o r*)[4] all existence (not yet softened through it) and is therefore terrible" (391).

Thus God needed sin and evil in order to reveal himself in existence.[5] Since sin consists in the elevation of man to the center, the truly good must consist in the submission by man of the dark principle of his selfhood to the periphery. Therefore, the human being cannot be the source of the bond of the truly good. Since the human being cannot create this bond, Schelling speaks of its being effected by "a divine magic," which he characterizes as "the immediate presence of being in consciousness and to knowledge" (391). In holding himself away from the center, the human being holds himself ready for the entrance of the divine magic. This "divine magic" is nothing other than the possibility of choosing being. This possibility was earlier called intellectual intuition, the experience of the immediate unity of being and knowing.

The whole as terrifying in sin becomes transfigured in the human being who is granted the vision of being. The human being cannot sustain this vision without aid. Schelling's ultimately unaccountable divine magic—like the sudden appearances of the Greek gods, the miracles in both Testaments, and the transport in the experience of sublimity in Kant's *Critique of Judgment*—helps the human being stand in being insofar as he can. The principles in evil are, of course, the same as those in good. The divine magic provides the aid that facilitates human effort to abide in the proper relation of the principles. Perhaps strangely, the problem in this section on the manifestation of evil is not how human beings come to choose evil. Rather, it concerns accounting for the possibility of the choice of the good principle in the face of humanity's tendency toward nonbeing. Yet the decision for good is no more arbitrary than the decision for evil:

> True freedom is in accord with a holy necessity of a sort we feel in the essential knowledge where spirit and heart, bound only through their own law, free-willingly affirm what is necessary. (391–92)

Through divine magic, the intelligibly grasped law is *felt* in the human spirit and the human heart. As the principles at work in freedom are the same as those in necessity, the divine magic instills a *holy* necessity as freedom's correlate. The decision for the good is nothing other than the free submission to this law, the accord of spirit (light) and heart (dark). Insofar as the unity of the two principles within humanity is God's self-revelation, the unfolding of the god within is simultaneously the unfolding of the god outside. Further, insofar as this unity is a bond of freedom in humanity, philosophical investigations that attend to the essence of human freedom unfold the whole by their very nature. They present the outline of the system of the world.

It may seem peculiar that the section on the manifestation of evil in man concludes with a rather detailed account of the manifestation of the bond of goodness in humanity. Schelling calls this bond *religiosity*, or conscientiousness (*Gewissenhaftigkeit*). However, the reality of evil is required for good to make itself manifest. Only through their struggle can goodness come to *life*. In this light, the section fulfills its task. In describing the manifestation of evil in humanity, it enables the *Freedom Essay* to show goodness as arising directly from its struggle with its false counterpart. The section moves in the very way the matter presents itself, namely the bond of the principles in evil serves to call forth the nature of their bond in true goodness.

Schelling distinguishes religiosity from both arbitrariness and self-determination. Arbitrariness has already been treated, and rather easily. In the system of the world, which is nothing different from freedom, there is no arbitrariness. "An arbitrary good is just as impossible as an arbitrary evil" (391). The distinction from self-determination is both more difficult and more important, for the latter is the Idealist determination of freedom. Kantian autonomy and Fichtean self-positing share this conception of freedom. Schelling questions the concept of self-determination in the following manner: "The [concept of self-determination] presupposed that 'the principles' were not in themselves, one; but how can they become one if they are not" (392)? This oneness in religiosity or conscientiousness is the very divine bond of the principles. This bond is prior to any division. The division issues from the unity, but the unity first comes to be discovered in human beings through its division.

The Idealist concept of freedom as self-determination fails to account for this original unity. Schelling employs Kant's conception of duty as Idealism's exemplar of self-determination. With the concept of *duty* in Kant serving as the exemplary case of the concept of freedom as self-determination, Schelling points out the tacit false duality implied in it:

> He is not conscientious who, in a given case, must first hold the command of duty before himself in order to decide to do right because of his respect for it. By the very meaning of the word, religiosity allows no choice between alternatives . . . but only the highest commitment to the right, without any choice. (392)

Thus, conscientiousness in humanity is that unity of knowledge (concept) and feeling that precludes any division. Whereas the concept of duty (if interpreted in Schelling's manner) serves to bind feeling to knowledge in an "ought," religiosity affirms the divine original bond of the two principles in humanity. Schelling's Kant interpretation assumes that desire and reason are two elements at odds in humanity. The moral law serves as a principle according to which the human being can lead himself to act rightly when pulled in two directions. The notion of *choice* in this Kantian sense only occurs in the absence of the divine bond. Schelling's notion of the unity of knowledge and feeling can properly be called an *instinct* for the good as the bond of the principles. "Instinct" here is another name for the god within.

The path from the god within to the god outside finds its first precise demarcation in the section on the manifestation of evil in man. The path might be seen as an ascent from the merely human to the divine. But this ascent is simultaneously a circling in which the human being returns to himself as he interprets himself. The unity of the human being with respect to himself is neither a real nor an ideal unity in this section. The necessary division of the principles in the human being is neither a barrier to the realization of an archetype, nor is any claim made that such a realization can occur. Beyond any such considerations, beyond optimism as well as pessimism, this section presents an interpretation of the human being that gives humanity to himself in an image of the whole as unified. One might call the human being the image of God without God.

The discussion of strictness of disposition (*Gesinnung*) with which the section closes distinguishes religiosity from enthusiasm of any kind. It also gives an interesting indication of the way in which the remainder of the work might be read. In critiquing Kant's concept of duty and attacking those who would make aesthetics the ground of ethics, Schelling indicates that the self-showing of the whole in humanity is fundamentally *serious*. Free affirmation of holy necessity requires the submission of self in man, an end of egoism. Only upon this serious self-submission can beautiful images of man—as hero, as faithful in the sense of trusting (*Republic* 603a)—be possible. The highest transfiguration of the moral life, however, is said to emerge in gracefulness (*Anmut*) and divine beauty, which occurs when the "inviolable seriousness of disposition receives a ray of divine love" (394). I note that seriousness is the necessary condition, and the ray of light serves as a means.

For a thinker who elevated art to as great a significance as any other in the history of philosophy, and who had great contemporaries who were kindred spirits in this area (I think particularly of Schiller), it is strange indeed that playfulness has little or no role.[6] Further, the entire *Freedom Essay* to this point at least tacitly if not openly displays and requires aesthetic sensitivity, and celebrates life in its erotic flowering. The sudden turn toward a primary seriousness jolts. In terms of the conceptual element, Schelling's earlier reading of *logismo notho* as "*false* imagination" becomes understandable, though hardly (in my view) tenable. Most surprising to me is that among modern thinkers, Schelling seems the best equipped to provide a creative and nonmoral appropriation of this phrase—perhaps as *Ahnung* (prescience).

The section on the manifestation of evil in man has shown that the revelation of falsehood is at once the revelation of truth. It has shown that the path through nonbeing is at once the path through being. It has shown that the path through evil is at once the path through goodness. With the remark that the highest transformation of the moral life emerges in grace and divine beauty, can one not discern the movement of the *Freedom Essay* as a movement through which the rigorously conceived whole becomes seen most profoundly as an *aesthetic* whole? And can one not therefore conclude that an image of humanity may be a vicarious image—a graceful and beautiful image? This calls to mind an image of Socrates, but perhaps not a Platonic one.

The much more serious Xenophon, in his *Symposium*, presents Socrates winning a contest in *logos* on beauty from the beautiful young Critobolus. He leads his interlocutor to define beauty as the quality of anything that is well designed for its purpose. Thus, Socrates' bulging eyes are more beautiful than Critobolus', since Socrates can see many sides while Critobolus can only see straight ahead. Similarly, Socrates' large nostrils enable him to smell more odors, his thick lips give him a sweeter kiss, and so on. Before the vote, Socrates shines a light on his own face, and on Critobolus.' (Critobolus is the unanimous victor.) In the divine magic of his conscientiousness, Socrates transfigures the hideous features with which he is marked, just as he honors the gift bestowed by the gods on Critobolus.[7]

VII

God as Moral Being—The Nature of the Whole with Respect to Freedom

THE SECTION FROM 394–406, as well as the concluding section on indifference, has been regarded by even so careful and sympathetic a reader as Heidegger as a more or less unfortunate appendix to a work that can be seen in many respects as complete without them. Indeed, the previous chapter points to the *Freedom Essay*'s coming full circle.

In Heidegger's view, "Schelling's original profundity and sharpness of metaphysical questioning fade away towards the conclusion."[1] He claims further, "The answer to the question of the justification of the absolute in view of evil has already been given previously."[2] Heidegger's study could not be further from a critique. As noted in the Introduction, he calls Schelling the most creative and farthest-reaching thinker of the age of German Idealism. His *Schelling* is largely a thinking celebration of the *Freedom Essay*. Indeed, this section seems to do nothing more than gather up the results of previous investigations and relate them to one another in terms of the Introduction. For example, it gives an explanation of the way the judgment "good and evil are the same" may be understood dialectically in terms of the findings of the investigations (400).

Despite this undeniable feature of the section, Schelling declares at its outset that "the highest question of this entire investigation is still not asked" (394). Schelling poses this question as that of the justification of God in the face of evil. This is most puzzling for two reasons: It is an old saw rather than a new question, and he has already answered it decisively. Evil is necessary for life and for goodness, for the birth of God and for the freedom of humanity to be real. But one cannot but wonder, precisely *because* the question seems to have been answered, whether indeed it has properly been heard. Far from weakening the sharpness of his questioning toward the end as Heidegger maintains, I suggest that Schelling poses the question of the justification of the absolute in the face of evil in a radically new way. The apparently external gathering of results may constitute a preparation for rethinking the nature of the whole, rather than a conclusion to what has come before and a relapse into traditional presuppositions. The shocking remark on system and life on 399 that I will soon consider indicates such an imminent rethinking.

For there is increased emphasis on a matter that has thus far been articulated mainly in terms of its place in the structure of the whole, namely *personality*. Schelling defines personality as selfhood elevated to spirituality in the human being. God, too, is personal: Spirituality becomes selfhood with respect to the birth of God. Until now it has seemed as if God himself is form and order requiring the will of the depths to come to life. Law occurs in the fold of God himself, considered apart from the ground of his existence. This way of presenting the twofold is neither changed nor contradicted in what will follow. Rather, the unity of the twofold as a onefold becomes enhanced when personality moves to the center.

> There are no consequences of universal laws, but God, that is the person of God, is the universal law, and everything that happens, happens by virtue of God's personality; not according to an abstract necessity which we could not bear in action, not to mention God. (396)

This remarkable passage lays the foundation for a radical transformation of the understanding of the whole as presented thus far in the *Freedom Essay*. The denial of any consequences to universal law is consistent with everything that has preceded this section: the simultaneity of the whole to itself, its unity as eternal, its showing in time as nothing other than the eternal giving birth to itself. What is different, however, is that *personality* is called universal law. Justice is nothing other than the unfolding of the whole, the undergoing of evil, the necessity of pain, death, and suffering. Fate, which God himself needed to undergo, is affirmed as justice. In terms of Schelling's logic, the identity of the law of identity and sufficient reason draws a limit to the principle of sufficient reason. To be sure, the sufficient reason for the undergoing of evil is the birth of good. The sufficient reason for the undergoing of death is the furtherance of life. There is, however, no sufficient reason for this sufficient reason. That is, there is no *sufficient* reason why the whole had to unfold through the pain of history. Although one may speak of a sufficient reason as to why life unfolded in the very way that it did (Schelling treats this in the final sections of the *Freedom Essay*), there is no sufficient reason for life. "God's person is the universal law": This says—behind personality one cannot find law, one cannot find sufficient reason.

Understood in this light, the section from 399–406 serves not merely to gather up but to redirect the results of the previous investigations. The investigations on the essence of human freedom have revealed the bond of freedom in humanity to consist of a unification of the principles that excludes all choice. It can be regarded as prior to all choice, so long as "prior" is not understood temporally but ontologically. The bond involves recognition of being bound to a condition neither of humanity's own making nor in the human being. These investigations thereby disclose an account of the bond of principles *in God* as prior to choice. The name of this bond is the personality of God.

Divine freedom excludes the possibility of choice. Thus, the coming to life of the whole is thoroughly unaccountable and unprovoked, neither chosen nor not chosen. Choice implies a distinction of possibility and actuality that does not occur in God. This opacity of life, certainly present throughout the *Freedom Essay*, moves more and more into consideration as the work nears its completion. It raises the questioning to a new height as it unfolds the dark depth lying at the root of all that has come before. The aforementioned shocking statement reads:

> In the divine understanding is a system, but God himself is no system, but rather a life, and therein alone lies the answer to the question for the sake of which this has been proposed, on account of the possibility of evil in relation to God. (399)

Heidegger asks: "What does system mean here?"[3] He notes further, "Here system is ascribed to only one moment of the structure of being (*Seynsfuge*), existence. At the same time a higher unity is posited and called 'life.'"[4] For Heidegger, this is the place at which Schelling regresses back to the tradition without creatively transforming it. He claims, "Schelling's use of language here is a 'polemical' one"[5] directed against the idealistic grasp of the absolute.

There are certainly grounds for interpreting Schelling in precisely this fashion. In the *Freedom Essay*, Schelling always insisted upon system as living. For him to declare suddenly that God is not a system but a life seems at odds with all that he has been at pains to establish in the previous investigations. However, there is another way of interpreting this astonishing remark. It accords with the unspoken movement of the *Freedom Essay*, which I have characterized as a series of provocations that drive the investigations into higher and deeper regions. It is another "contradiction" necessary for a higher manifestation of spirit. This will be demonstrated especially in the final section on indifference. There, it will not only demonstrate the underlying unity of the entire work, but will point to a creative transformation of the tradition as well.

The above-cited passage indeed affirms that system occurs in the divine understanding, but the passage also distinguishes God himself from system. Previously, however, understanding was placed on the side of God himself (359–60). "God" meant God as existing, distinguished from the ground of his existence. The shift, therefore, need not occur as a shift in the meaning of system, as Heidegger maintains. There may rather be a shift in the understanding of *God himself*. Here, God himself is understood as personality, unity of selfhood and spirit (ground and existence) rather than as mere existence. As Schelling explains, "All existence demands a condition, in order that it may become actual, namely personal existence" (399). This statement leads to the following inference: Schelling's words claiming that God himself is not a system but a life may not disjoin God from system. Nor do they place system merely on the side of existence. Rather, they affirm the condition without which anything such as system can occur at all. That is, system is still the living whole of the *hen panta* but can be such only by virtue of conditioned personality. Further, Schelling has said that the understanding is nothing other than the will in willing. This affirms the unity of understanding and will of the depths. Therefore, to attribute system to the divine understanding need not imply its exclusion from the ground. In this light, the fundamental matter addressed in Schelling's provocative remark is the irreducible unaccountability of life, which system articulates in its wholeness.

In the earlier investigations, the *Freedom Essay* disclosed the intimate relation of the system of the whole with human freedom. The task of this section is to interpret the whole as life in light of the earlier investigations. In this regard, something that implicitly provided depth throughout comes forth in this section, namely the *finitude of God*:

> God's existence too could not be personal if there were not such a condition, only he has the condition *in* himself, not outside himself. He

> cannot overcome or cancel (*aufheben*) the condition, insofar as in so doing he would have to cancel himself; he can only overpower it through love and subordinate it to his glorification. (399)

The life of the whole occurs, then, as the overcoming of the condition. Schelling presents this overcoming in personal terms, as victory in the struggle between the will to revelation and the will of the depths. ". . . Where there is no struggle, there is no life" (400). The victory does not consist of eliminating the depths, which remain a necessary element of that struggle. Rather, the victory consists in bringing the depths to unity with the will to revelation. The site of the struggle is humanity: Human freedom as the power for good and evil. The human struggle with respect to fate, which is the condition outside of humanity, yields human personality. By contrast, the divine life is personal also by virtue of overcoming the condition. The difference is that the condition is within God rather than outside him.

The condition necessary for personality can never fully be mastered in the human being. "Hence his personality and self can never be raised to complete actuality" (399). Since the personality of the human being can never entirely overcome the condition, there is "an inherent sorrow (*Traurigkeit*) in all finite life . . . hence the veil of sadness (*Schwermuth*) that is spread over all nature, the deep, indestructible (*unzerstörliche*) melancholy of all life"[6] (399). This sadness concerns the inability to become fully personal. It is not a lament about being given over to death.[7]

For there is a source of sadness as well in God "which, however, never attains actuality but rather serves for the eternal joy and triumph" (399). However, the *human* struggle serves as the image of the whole in which the condition is subdued through love. Sadness and joy issue from the division of the principles that constitute the human condition. To say that love is necessary even for God to surmount one of the conditions is to say that God also is in need, is finite. However "we do deny that finitude in itself is evil" (370). The distinction between evil and finitude is the hidden depth of the answer to the question of the justification of God in the face of evil. Further, the distinction points ahead to a rethinking of the whole as finite and living.

To the question as to whether evil ends, to whether creation has a final purpose, to why perfection was not achieved at the beginning, Schelling writes:

> *There is no answer* to this except the one already given: because God is a life, not merely a being. All life, however, has a destiny, and is subject to suffering and becoming. (403, emphasis mine)

However, this destiny is nothing prior to the development of the whole. Final purpose conceived as "a distant future when God will be all in all" (404) is merely a temporal representation of the destiny of the whole.

> For this is the final purpose of creation, that that which could not be for itself, is for itself, insofar as it is raised into existence (*Dasein*) out of the darkness, as a ground independent of God. (404)

In other words, the final purpose of creation is nothing other than creation, nothing other than the birth of God, nothing other than life. Final purpose is not, considered for itself, a beyond or a future, however distant. It pertains only to time-bound humanity.

In yet another shocking statement, Schelling speaks of an end of revelation. He calls it "the expulsion of the evil from the good, the explanation of it as entire unreality" (405). Again, this looks like a clear contradiction in light of his decisive rejection of Scholasticism in the earlier investigations. Scholastic theodicy accounted for evil by denying its reality. Schelling's definition of the essence of human freedom as the capacity for good and evil, with evil having just as much reality as goodness, directly contravenes the Scholastic attribution of nonbeing to evil. However, I read this as another Schellingeian provocation.

Read carefully, the words say that the *explanation* (*Erklärung*) of the unreality of evil constitutes its banishment. The meaning of "explanation" here is crucial. Interpreted in context, it exhibits Schelling's stance at the dividing line of German Idealism and beyond. In one sense, *Erklärung* means "bringing to the clarity of light" in the word, in the living word. In this way and only in this way can history be comprehended, that is, brought to concepts: "All history remains incomprehensible without the concept of a humanly suffering God . . ." (403–4). The Christian God as the word become flesh, undergoing becoming and passing away, is that clarity in which the darkness of human suffering and sin become redeemed. In terms of the tradition, "redeemed" means "brought to clarity."

Redemption, the separating off of the evil from the good in death, is seen as the end of life and thus as the end of history as revelation. This means that revelation, bringing to light, is by its very nature good. The will to concealment, the will to master revelation and keep it for oneself (the will to darkness in humanity) is by nature evil. This is the response to the early provocation that the philosopher keeps his understanding pure and undarkened by evil. Since the philosopher is the one to whom *logos* is entrusted and makes the whole manifest, then *logos* is revelatory by its nature and therefore good. Revealed evil is no longer evil. And in this sense philosophy may be seen as the unlimited uncovering of the whole, as a purification of falsehood through the presentation of the unfolding of truth. In such a reading, one can certainly discern an orientation toward transparency in Schelling, with even the opacity of life becoming clarified (explained) in the light of *logos*. This would indeed vindicate Heidegger's criticism.

However, there is another way to understand *Erklärung* and the purgation of evil as the end of revelation. The unreality of evil asserts only the dialectical sameness of good and evil: what is real in evil is goodness. Without goodness, evil would have no actuality. The undergoing of evil is by nature good, since without this undergoing for the sake of the revelation, evil would have triumphed. If evil triumphed, concealment and darkness would be the victors. Consequently, there would be nothing at all. Something beyond this dialectical sameness is required to show the purgation of evil. Schelling writes:

> Therefore, for the realization of the idea of a finite, all-sided perfection, a reestablishment of evil into good (the return of all things) is in no sense required; because the evil is only evil insofar as it goes beyond potentiality; reduced to non-being, or to the condition of potency, it is what it is always supposed to be—basis, subjected, and as such no longer in contradiction with the holiness nor the love of God. (405)

Thus, just as one might speak of God with respect only to his existence as God-not-yet-God, one might speak of evil merely with respect to its potential as evil-not-yet-evil. And as God first becomes God in the unification of existence and ground, evil is only evil insofar as it shows itself in life through its effects. There is, however, this crucial difference, that with the subordination of evil the basis yet remains, whereas in the subordination of good nothing at all can be.

Thus, the idea of all-sided perfection (the purgation of evil) is bound to the idea of finitude (*endlich*—final as finite). This basis is needed in order for the good to show itself both as good and as triumphant over evil. A second sense of *Erklärung* is closer to the Greek sense of *muthologia*. It speaks to the way this very showing is simultaneously a purgation of evil and a preservation of the dark basis necessary for revelation. I think here of this showing as an *imaging*, which enacts this purgation precisely by setting the dark basis back into itself.

Images join being and nonbeing. In order for something to be seen, a twofoldness is required. This twofold may be represented as darkness and light, as of light and gravity, or of *hule* and *paradeigma* ("*matter*" and "*paradigm*") as in Plato's *Timaeus*. Such twofolds empowered the unfolding of nature as the unfolding of the divine in the depths, and the unfolding of humanity as the unfolding of the divine in history. Further as we have seen, the divine is nothing other than this very unfolding. It is nothing other than the whole come to life. In this sense humanity is the image of God, but it is *an image without an original*. The "original" is itself an image drawn up by the human being in terms of which the whole may be conceived *as* whole. Thus, the revelation of God is identical with the whole understood as image.

What then of evil and its purification? Evil is not evil if it remains subordinated, reduced to nonbeing. In humanity, only elevated selfhood is evil. So long, then, as the human being understands himself as *not* being the center but rather understands himself *as* an image, evil remains sealed off into potentiality. The purgation of evil, in the more profound sense, precisely involves this *seeing of an image as an image*. Such insight seals off the desire to take over the center (to act as original). Such insight seals off evil as evil. In an image seen as an image, there is nonbeing but no evil. The understanding of image as image, therefore, is simultaneously the preservation of the twofold of being and nonbeing, the banishment of evil. Revelation is by nature good, and revelation occurs as imaging. Thus, revelation remains bound to nonbeing in this way.

According to this view, the understanding of creation as a moral act no longer applies. With the purgation of evil in interpreting images as images, a purgation of good in the moral sense must also occur. Moreover, the initial provocation of this alternative interpretation, according to which the person of God is universal law, must be further transformed. If (1) creation is its own end, and (2) the end of revelation is the victory of good as clarification of the unreality of evil, and (3) the unreality of evil is clarified in the nature of imaging, then creation must be seen in terms of something prior even to good and evil and other than good and evil. This "other" constitutes the subject matter of the final section.

This second sense of *logos* in Schelling points to the whole as aesthetic whole. This meaning has pervaded my reading throughout, and is justified by this alternative interpretation. However, with the transformation of the understanding of creation from a moral to an artistic act, a transformation in the understanding of justice and justification must likewise occur. Since God's person is the universal law without consequences, justice must be seen not in terms of morality, but in terms of a meting out of artistic measure in the play of images. The whole, and humanity, must come to be understood and justified as works of art . . . without artists. The laws of art are alone without consequences. This factor might make them the most terrifying laws of all, more so than any moral commandment could ever be.

However, it cannot be denied that there is a moral sense to the unfolding of the whole in Schelling. After all, this chapter's title speaks of God as a moral being, and at least seems to unfold in a language of theodicy—albeit a peculiar one. I suggest that Schelling's sense of the moral cannot but cross over into the aesthetic, where images of gods and heroes rule in the place of laws. To conclude by picturing Schelling as standing at a dividing line with one foot in the tradition and the other beyond it may have scholarly justification, but it would miss the deepest depths of Schelling's thought and so miss a rare opportunity. For the very twofoldness of the unfolding of the whole, as *moral* and as *aesthetical*, is itself an image of the unfolding of the whole. It reveals a play of goodness and beauty in which the two are gathered and yet held apart. The twofoldness of moral and aesthetical is at once moral, aesthetical, and an image. As such, it constitutes the whole in a way appropriate to the needful nature of humanity. Perhaps in this unspoken twofoldness that animates the entirety of the *Freedom Essay*, one can discern what likely may have happened when Greek and modern met, and can find much in that meeting that still and always requires a hearing.

Indifference and the Birth of Love

THE PREVIOUS INVESTIGATION took a different path than its predecessors. In Schelling's words, it approached the *Freedom Essay*'s "highest" level of questioning. It presented God not merely as system but as life. This appeared to contradict the view of the whole as living system that Schelling had so carefully developed. However, this contradiction can be read as a provocation, like so many of Schelling's statements throughout the *Freedom Essay*. In taking up the provocation of Schelling's presentation, I interpreted it as the fruition of the view of the whole that points toward a unity of the moral and the aesthetic that is prior to both. This prior unity opens the way to a different understanding of origin and of difference. Of this section Heidegger has written:

> Also here Schelling does not see the necessity of an essential step. If being in truth cannot be said of the absolute, this lies in that the essence of all being is finitude and that only finite existence has the privilege and the pain to stand in being and to experience the true as being.[1] (*Seiendes*)

There is no quarrel regarding the necessity of this step. I have endeavored to show that the step has indeed occurred in Schelling. From this step, indifference as the highest point can be understood.

Insofar as the unification of the principles is in its highest sense an erotic unity, love may be seen as highest. Love is above even spirit, which love unifies with the depths. However, it is only in the deed of unifying the principles that love first is love.[2] And yet love is "that which was there before the ground and before the existing were (as divided), but was there not yet as *Love*, but rather—how shall we designate it" (406)?

The answer to this question requires apprehending the origin before all unification as well as before all duality. Can it be said that the origin is present as concealed in all duality and unification? (One might here recall Phaedrus' remark toward the beginning of Plato's *Symposium* regarding the rarity of speeches in praise of *eros*, and the plethora of speeches about all the other gods.)

However, bringing this origin to *logos* would seem to falsify its character as origin. For *logos* by its nature brings together as it holds apart, gathers and divides. The origin is antecedent to both unity and separation. This is why Schelling writes that love was "there" before all division and unity of the principles, but not as love (as unifying). Further and significantly, this is why a hesitation occurs ("it was not there as love—how shall we designate it?"). This is also why the designation of the origin is a question, a problem. Yet at the same time, the origin *must* be brought to *logos*, in order to bring the investigations to the systematic completeness required. But again, the origin, as outside all considerations of one and many, is outside all consideration of system as *hen panta*. Yet if there is no origin, there can be no system.

Given the opacity belonging to this matter, one can well understand why Schelling speaks of this highest point prior even to love in negative terms: It is not primal ground or ground at all but *un*ground. As it excludes antitheses, it is *in*difference. Its only predicate is predicate*less*ness. But it is not nothing, nor is it an un-thing (406). There are two striking features of Schelling's account of indifference. First, Schelling brings indifference to *logos* in such a way that all elements of judgment and thought are barred: no predicates, neither being nor nothing. Even more interestingly, this way of speaking renders impossible the deed of forming any image whatsoever of the groundless, yet there is no contradiction in its conception. Both being and nonbeing belong to an image. Yet neither can be predicated of the groundless (indifference), nor can either of the two be denied of it. However, Schelling goes on to say,

> Reality and ideality, darkness and light, or however else we wish to designate the two principles can never be predicated of the groundless as *antitheses*; but nothing prevents their being predicated as non-antitheses, that is, in disjunction and each *for itself*, with which, however, just this duality (the actual twofoldness of the principles) is posited. (407)

How indeed can one designate this peculiar indifference, which itself has no predicates but which allows of non-antithetical predication? Ironically, the most appropriate "designation" of the groundless occurs in Heidegger's *Schelling* treatise. The irony has two dimensions. First, Heidegger did not discern this character of the indifference in Schelling although there are ample resources in his own thought. Also, Heidegger points out in several places there that great thinkers frequently misunderstand one another in often shocking ways (this observation pertained particularly to Hegel's treatment of Schelling's thought). That is, indifference—as the neither-nor from which all unity and wholeness breaks forth and to which everything owes its presence, but which is not itself present—sounds like nothing other than the *clearing* (*Lichtung*) of which Heidegger speaks, in which withdrawal gives to thinking its matter.

It is by virtue of that neither-nor of the groundless that anything like a *showing*, an image, can burst forth. For a two-ness of some kind is required for any showing, however this two-ness be conceived. Only by virtue of a "groundless," or a "clearing," can two principles occur, each for themselves. Each member is distinct and separate from the other. Schelling's word *disjunction* is well chosen, so long as it is not understood in the dead formal-logical sense as a sum of all possibilities, or in the ordinary sense of exclusion. The groundless then confirms the twofoldness of principles, but neither as a dualism nor as a unity. Since the two principles are gathered in the indifference without any concept (unifier), their togetherness is a separateness—or rather they must be understood as neither by nature separate nor by nature together. "Two" and "one" function as "numbers-not-yet-numbers."

Schelling's "dialectical exposition" is followed by an explanation (*Erklärung*) that is totally determinate. It is intended to present the whole in its character as whole, to present *hen panta* (one is all) as *hen* and as *panta*. The *unground* is called the absolute considered directly. That is, the absolute will not be considered in terms of those earlier negative determinations that do not have correspondingly positive ones. Both principles can be predicated of it, so that it is both "not *at the same time*, but that it is in both *in the same way*, as the whole in each, or a unique essence" (408). In this sense, both principles are eternal (independent of time) and whole, with each having its own individuality and integrity. The unground is wholly in each in the sense that in its total withdrawal (as indifference), both principles can emerge as distinct and different. But with the withdrawal of the unground as the "self-division into two equally eternal beginnings" (408), indifference is no longer indifference: "But the unground divides itself . . . only in order that (*nur damit*) the two which could not be in it as unground at the same time or be one, should become one through love, i.e., it divides itself only that there may be life and love and personal existence" (408).[3]

The occurrence of the whole as living whole is reconceived in this concluding section as the birth of love out of indifference. This latter image seals the radical unaccountability of the whole. For in this account, love bursts forth from nothing and for no reason. In this regard the birth of love images the very way *eros* appears in the human being—suddenly, at no time, for no reason, transforming everything. Life and love and personality owe their existence to the unground. But there is no creditor. Life, love, and personality occur to humanity as fate.

Only through love can the two principles—each existing for itself, yet needing one another to be at all—occur *at the same time* (since in the unground as unground they cannot be predicated with respect to time). Therefore, both the simultaneous as well as the successive natures of the whole are owed to love. Since the human being is the one to whom and in whom the whole occurs fully, love hands time over to humanity from which it gleans the timeless. So not only the eternal but also the temporal is *mythical*, a likely account of life. In this regard, Schelling's account of indifference and the birth of love is a tale of the origin of time mythologized out of the radical unaccountability of the whole. In Heideggerian terms, thought of the clearing is granted from within the clearing in which the human being finds himself.

Thus, if spirit is the nexus of the principles and love may rule as their nexus, there is something higher than spirit, namely love. Love first occurs as not-yet-love but as the unground. "But beyond the spirit is the initial unground, which is no longer indifference (neutrality), but however is not the identity of the two principles, but rather the general unity, the same to all yet partisan to nothing, free from all yet the beneficence working through all with One Word—love, which is all in all" (408).

With this, the unground is interpreted as beneficence, as *agape*. *Agape* here is that love which is not the unification of opposites out of struggle. Rather, it is the gentle repose from which all struggle must emerge in order to understand itself as struggle, that is, to experience itself as life. *Agape* gives itself up as *agape* for the sake of life. To say, then, that love is the all in all is to say that the absolute as *agape* shows itself in the living whole as the unifier of opposites. It pulls together all things into a harmony and thereby triumphs over the spirit of discord. But the absolute as love is concealed in the whole. Heraclitus' thought always seems to breathe beneath the surface of the *Freedom Essay*. Here, another fragment sounds out of its depths: "*harmonin aphanes phaneres kreitton* (an unappearing harmony is stronger than an appearing one)."[4] Schelling's notion of indifference as free beneficence points to the power of the unapparent harmony. It empowers the apparent *harmonia* to shine, as well as the discords necessary for the shining harmonies to shine.

The withdrawal occurs for the human being in several ways. It occurs as the difference from himself of the condition of his existence (ignorance). It occurs as pain and the inability to master the condition (sadness). It occurs as incompleteness (partiality). However, the difference that announces the division of the principles also discloses the whole within which they divide. The solicitation to evil that brings human freedom to life makes possible the vision of the subordination of the condition through reason and imagination. It also provokes the desire in the human being to fashion this twofold revelation into an intelligible whole, whether rational, aesthetical, or a joining of the two. That is, it provokes the desire to fashion a system. In other words, the withdrawal calls forth *philosophy*, engages the *eros* of the philosopher. In philosophy, the whole can be presented as the system of freedom. In the system, the ignorance as well as the vision, the sadness as well as the joy becomes joined into a whole. The system of freedom is a *vicarious* whole, a living image. And in this way, the whole receives measure, determinacy, by the very deed of its being brought to *logos*. There is only one system, the system of the world, and in this regard the deed of system-making at once images and is imaged by the one system. As Schelling writes in *Concerning the Nature of Philosophy as Science*:

> . . . All experiencing, feeling, seeing is in and for itself mute, and required a mediating organ in order to succeed to expression. If this is lacking to the one who sees, or he intentionally pushes it away from himself in order to discourse immediately from his vision, he loses the measure necessary to him. . . .[5]

Neither the philosopher, nor the vision, nor reason, nor the whole, nor the willful deed of speech can serve as the measure. Rather, in an unaccountable way, system as the whole brought to its mediating organ (*logos*) gives measure to what is otherwise measureless. The articulation of system draws up the measure for itself. As the system of freedom unfolded in *logos*, so too did the limits belonging to the human being. The human being is essentially subject to an essential division within himself, and is therefore never complete with respect to himself. The human being can never attain to full personality, because he cannot fully master the condition to which he has been given over. The human being requires aid even to overcome solicitation to evil tempting him to elevate his particular will over the universal. The philosopher, able to conceive the god outside him with the god within him, must speak in a manner suitable to the dark depths as well as to the principle of light: bringing *muthos* and *logos* together, *mythologia*, mythologizing. Philosophical speaking recognizes itself as cut off from the condition, precluded from bringing originals directly to speech. Accordingly, Schelling takes mythology and religion as essential sources of vicarious *images* of and for humanity.

The remainder of the *Freedom Essay* occupies itself with the nature of philosophy in general and with its connection to religion and mythology. The account of indifference points toward both the source of and the goad to philosophy. The source is our distance from wisdom, and the goad is also our distance from wisdom. We find this distance imaged in the division of the principles in us. The division of the principles reveals the condition (the depths) that we can never fully overcome. However, the experience of this division makes possible the vision and the presentation of the system of the whole. In this vision and presentation, one principle holds for and permeates all: *hen kai pan*.

Schelling acknowledges the possibility of his system being construed in many ways: as pantheism, as affirming the lifeless sameness of good and evil, and as regarding God as abstract rather than personal. For all these falsifications of the system are possibilities *of* the system, that is, ways of construing the whole. They might be called *aspects* or partial sightings of the system. However, the system itself is not properly understood unless the interplay of the various aspects is taken to heart, that is, the *life* of the system is understood and taken to heart. Thus, all accounts based upon such aspects may assert something correct without asserting something true, or *truly* true. In Schelling's system, then, the occurrence of truth points beyond the notion of truth as correctness toward a more fundamental sense of truth as *revelation*. In relation to truth as revelation, truth as correctness is its mere secondary manifestation. In this regard, the objections that Schelling answers and the alternatives he addresses are not attacked for their incorrectness but for their incomplete apprehension of what is shown in them.

Considered in terms of the *Freedom Essay*, both the objections and the alternatives fail to see how the philosophical deed of system building belongs to the system that is built. Schelling's system presents the whole in its living unity. But it does so out of the fragmentation to which the philosopher is given over. From this fragmentation, the philosopher can discern and articulate the deeply concealed unity in a system. But the philosopher can do so without taking it over, that is, by mindfully preserving its deeply concealed character. The philosopher recognizes the limit of this deed. The building of a philosophical system does not involve the pretense of overcoming human needfulness and distance from himself, but rather confirms it. In making good its lack (*muthos*), it recognizes the limits and the nature of this "making good."

Of the division of man from himself as recognized by the philosopher, Schelling has written in *The Worldages*:

> This distinction, this doubling of ourselves, this secret commerce in which there are two beings, a questioning and an answering, and unknowing who, however, seeks knowledge (*Wissenschaft*) and a knowing who, however, does not know his knowing—this silent conversation, this inner art of dialogue, the proper secret of the philosopher, is that of which the outer, namely dialectic, therefore, is the afterimage, and where it has become mere form, is the empty semblance and shadow.[6]

This should not be interpreted to mean that language is the external expression of (internal) thought for Schelling. The path of Schelling's work as it has been traced through the *Freedom Essay* makes such an interpretation unlikely. Rather, the passage recalls key moments in two Platonic dialogues.

First, from the *Sophist*: "Aren't thought (*dianoia*)[7] and speech (*logos*) the same, except that what we call thought is speech that occurs without the voice, inside the soul in conversation (*dialogos*) with itself: *d i a n o i a*" (263e2–5)? The citation above does not privilege inner dialogue over its external presentation in dialectic. Rather, when dialectic becomes *mere* form instead of living form, dialectic becomes the shadow instead of the incorporation of form that actually *forms*. From the myth of Theuth and Thamus in the *Phaedrus*:

> [Writing] will introduce forgetfulness into the souls of those who learn it: they will not practice using their memory (*mnemes*) because they will put their trust in writing, which is external and depends on signs that belong to others, instead of trying to remember from inside, completely on their own. You have not discovered a potion (*pharmakon*) for remembering (*hupomneseos*), but for recollecting (*anamimneskomenous*). You provide your students with the semblance of wisdom, not with true wisdom. (275a2–7)

The written word is not itself primary, and can surely mislead. However, it also serves to provoke *recollection*, the appropriate deed of the soul (see *Meno* 81c5–e2). In Schellingian terms, science (written philosophy) must be seen as the provocation of that inner, living dialogue that discloses the human being to himself and to the whole. Just as the clash of arms in the struggle of good and evil conceals the free, gentle beneficence at the source of all, the verbal polemic between philosophical systems conceals the silence from which all language springs and for the sake of which the polemic occurs.

In the midst of a polemical footnote mentioned in the introduction to this book, Schelling writes:

> The course that the author has taken in the present essay where, although the external form of dialogue is lacking, nevertheless everything emerges in the manner of a conversation, he will also retain in the future. Much here could have been more sharply determined and less loosely presented, much could more expressly have been preserved from misinterpretation. In part, the author failed to do so intentionally.[8] (410n)

The presentation of the system in the *Freedom Essay*, then, is in part designed to provoke the genuine inner dialogue. It sets forth the system, but requires a deed of thinking in order to appropriate what has been said. The reader must be interlocutor rather than acolyte. In this way, the life spoken of as so basic to the *Freedom Essay* is awakened in the active thought of the reader. Regarding polemics, Schelling is clear: "the artificial corkscrew twists of polemical writing cannot, after all, be the true form of philosophy" (335).

This citation appears in his own Introduction. But his Introduction could hardly be more polemical. Similarly, the above footnote containing his claim that the *Freedom Essay* proceeds dialogically is itself quite confrontational. He accuses many authors of "unmanly pantheistic drivel (*Schwindel*)." He says of those who produce other systems that "nature denied [them] intelligence in even everyday affairs, [yet they] believe themselves called upon to join in philosophizing" (410n). Here, I suggest, is another Schellingian provocation. Polemics belong to the human struggle. Yet they also point back to the silent beneficence that grants the possibility of all discord as well as all harmony. The philosopher comprehends their role in the whole. That is, the philosopher understands these polemics as belonging to the play of images.

Philosophy can occur as polemic because the impulse to philosophize does not occur strictly as reason. "Only in personality is there life; and all personality rests on a dark ground which must, to be sure, therefore also be ground of knowledge" (413). The dark ground of personality in man is manifest as feeling, which stirs the human being. The feeling of freedom is the point of departure for this work. Thus, feeling too belongs to the impulse to philosophize. Schelling writes in *The Worldages*:

> The human being rejuvenates himself (*verjüngt sich*) again and again and becomes newly blissful through the feeling of the unity of his essence. In precisely this, the constantly fresh science-seeking power is particularly creative; not only the poet but also the philosopher has his raptures. He requires them, so that through the feeling of the indescribable reality of those higher representations he may be protected from the forceful concept of an empty and spiritless dialectic.[9]

In the *Freedom Essay*, Schelling speaks of these raptures as *inspiration*. As the active combination of the two principles in spirit, inspiration is "the effective principle of each productive creative art or science" (414). Philosophy has its own "genuinely scientific" (414) inspiration. In this inspiration, the dark depths of feeling unite with the heights of reason and understanding. In the unity of the philosophical inspiration, the meeting of modern and Greek philosophy in Schelling's *Freedom Essay* can most clearly be discerned.

To be sure, the demand for a system of reason occurs as the dominant feature of modern thought first detailed by Kant. Schelling's scientific inspiration led him to its creative appropriation and transformation of Kant's systematic thought. Schelling articulated the nature of the whole from a single principle that contains the way of its unfolding within itself. This transformation required the incorporation of mythical speaking into its rational counterpart, in order to account for the dark depths necessary for both the appearance and the life of the whole. Scientific inspiration also recalls the divine madness of which Socrates speaks in Plato's *Phaedrus* (243e11–245c5). He specifies four noble deeds that owe their outcome to divine madness: prophesy, relief from plagues, possession by the Muses, and *eros*.[10] Socrates's famous words to his gifted pupil Theaetetus in the eponymous dialogue also resound here: ". . . for this feeling (*pathos*) of wonder (*thaumazein*) shows that you are a philosopher, since wonder is the one and only (*e haute*) origin (*arche*) of philosophy" (155d2–4). In Schelling, divine madness is taken up as philosophical rapture. This rapture is nothing opposed to reason, just as the dark depths in themselves are not opposed to goodness.

What role does philosophical rapture play in Schelling's thought? Most importantly, the rapture acknowledges the nonhuman origin of philosophy. The human being requires a spark not of his own design in order to begin philosophizing. In Schelling's transformed notion of divine madness, the powers with which one has to work and the solicitation to evil that actuates the powers are *given* to the human being. It is not our destiny to change them in any way. However, our freedom directs them in a certain way. We are our own acts, although we are not our own origin. In this regard, the philosophical inspiration carries within it a recognition of the limits of humanity. Philosophy can therefore occur in many ways, as a critique of pure reason, as a dialogue appealing to a restraint-counseling *daimonion*, as a series of cryptic investigations into the essence of human freedom.

Perhaps the most remarkable feature of the penultimate paragraph of the *Freedom Essay* is Schelling's characterization of reason:

> Reason in humanity is . . . initial (*anfängliche*) wisdom in which all things are together yet severed, [all things are] One and yet each is free in its own way. It is not activity as spirit, not absolute identity of both principles of knowledge, but rather indifference; the measure and at the same time (*gleichsam*) the universal place of truth, the restful abode wherein original wisdom is received, according to which the understanding, gazing at its primal image (*Urbild*), should image (*nach welcher, als dem Urbild hinblickend, der Verstand bilden soll*).[11] Philosophy has its name, on the one hand, from love as the universally inspiring principle, and on the other from this original wisdom that is its actual goal. (415)

In its most original sense, for Schelling, reason is neither the faculty of mediate inference nor the faculty of principles (*Prinzipien*), as in Kant. Rather, reason is an image of the source in which all wisdom rests. That is, reason is a beautiful image of the origin in relation to which man is both distant and near. Thus, reason itself is pulled into the unaccountable whole that, after a fashion, it measures.

Reason in humanity is indifference? This also pulls reason back into contact with its Greek ancestry. The striving of the understanding to image its primal image hearkens back to the Platonic *muthologia* in the *Meno*, "all knowledge is recollection." Socrates first presents this saying in a myth of Pindar affirming the immortality of the soul.[12] The encounter with Meno's slave boy follows, in which Socrates leads the boy to a result that we know we cannot precisely know (the square root of 3).[13] In this way, both key turning points of Greek philosophy and their modern counterparts draw together in the unique thought of Schelling, in whom Kant's rigorous critiques meet Plato's just as rigorous play.

Conclusion

CIRCLING BACK

IN THE INTRODUCTION, I raised four questions concerning the relation of Schelling's thought in the *Freedom Essay* to matters confronting philosophy today. The preceding study suggests the following answers/hints.

To (1): *For Schelling, the presence of both philosophy and the world as* systematic *is virtually assumed as given. Why? Why has system fared so poorly in recent and contemporary philosophy?* An answer can be found in the general view that Western metaphysics can no longer speak our philosophical language, and system-building belongs to Western metaphysics. This view has been so widespread that it has become the conventional wisdom. It takes effort to recover the living impulses that first gave rise to what is rapidly becoming commonplace. The work of Nietzsche and Heidegger has exposed its weaknesses and unexamined presuppositions to the point that we simply cannot philosophize in this manner any longer. Derrida has added his influential voice. Sallis speaks often of "philosophy at the limit," that is, as taking place at the end of metaphysics.

However, especially in Sallis' work, resources for thought are located, explored, and freshly interpreted in what is too easily regarded as "the history of philosophy," that is, as a series of important books. It belongs to the strength and the honor of contemporary Continental philosophy that these "books" are opened up as if for the first time, or rather are allowed to speak *to us* as the discovered depth of ourselves as we attempt not only to think through what presses upon us, but to decide—amidst the disorder that reigns—precisely what it is that does so.

Schelling presupposed what we would deny, namely that philosophy is by nature systematic. However, Schelling also fought for a living and positive philosophy, of which system is its expression. Schelling's system evolves in large measure through a sustained dialogue with the history of philosophy, which lives fully in every genuine philosophical thought. System creatively appropriates the living history of philosophy, recollecting the life from which it springs but has remained concealed in its depth. The hold of system in this living and positive sense, in an ever-renewing Heraclitean *hen panta*, has loosened considerably—perhaps to the point that we are scarcely aware of it.

To (2): *For Schelling, the logical copula expressed a living relation. Logic is thought most fundamentally in terms of the Greek* logos. *Why? How has the copula, and how has logic in general, come to be conceived and interpreted as formal?* Kant's critical philosophy serves as a source for Anglo-American philosophy as well as for our Continental counterpart. Since Kant's originary logic is transcendental, incorporating pure intuition as part of its fabric, this makes the reduction of logic to its most formal aspect all the more deplorable and inexplicable. Schelling's daring recovery of what he calls "the ancient logic" creatively appropriates Kant's originary logic, while his analytic "heirs" limp along ineptly in inverse proportion to their influence in America and England.

How has the logical copula, called by Kant the *Verhältniswörtchen* "is," come to be understood as merely formal? Heidegger speaks of the forgetfulness of being, and claims that German Idealism came to an end not because of any inherent weakness, but because the age was not strong enough to sustain it. I have no quarrel whatsoever with either of these thoughts. I would only add something more mundane, namely that philosophy is a difficult subject.

To (3): *For Schelling, darkness resides at the heart of all disclosure as its living basis. The role of concealment in all disclosure has been, since Heidegger, widely acknowledged and considered. What might Schelling's* Freedom Essay *add to this consideration?* I suggest that Schelling's darkness—ground as will, longing, unruliness—remains our own. To Nietzsche's will to power and to Heideggerian concealment, Schellingian darkness recollectively adds the pull of that necessity "which sets things adrift (*he pherein pephuken*—*Timaeus* 48a9)." Schelling reminds that this "errant" element is the living basis of all articulation. Whenever we speak, our language lives and breathes errancy in order to be language at all.

Schelling's thought of the remainder that can never be contained (*der nie aufgehende Rest*) (359–60) speaks to us with special resonance. As discussed earlier, this "remainder" is hardly something "left over" from the ground's function of grounding. Rather, it names the character of the unruly itself. As a thinker attuned to his time, Schelling never abandons rule, order, and form as world characteristics. (Perhaps we should not abandon these too quickly, either.) As an untimely thinker, he is attuned as well to the dark subsoil beneath the surfaces upon which we tread.

To (4): *For Schelling, divine experience is an ever-ongoing presence. In Anglo-American philosophy, such talk is an embarrassment. In Continental philosophy, God is present in an oblique fashion, if at all. Can Schelling's thought be brought into fruitful dialogue with either or both?* Leaving our analytic colleagues to their serene sophistication for a moment, material for dialogue with Continental philosophy abounds in the *Freedom Essay*, where one finds a subtle unfolding of divine finitude even in a context where Christianity plays a significant role.

Many thinkers in our philosophy address the post-Holocaust thought of God, most notably Levinas and Derrida. In light of their work, it may sound peculiar indeed to speak of the triumph of the good and of "the beneficence working through all with One Word—love, which is all in all" (408).

Here I can only gesture haltingly toward how these especially untimely words might enter our contemporary discussion. Might not the absence and its attendant mourning be thought out of the beneficence as *its* now concealed darkness?

SCHELLING REVIVAL

This part of the conclusion will be substantially less formal than its predecessor. I am finished elucidating textual matters concerning the *Freedom Essay* as such. Here, I offer opinions on the recent Schelling revival. Some are sober. Some are somewhat freewheeling. Others are personal. Still others, toward the end, address the possible and actual role of Schelling's thought in contemporary Continental philosophy.

Book titles rarely provide the opportunity for protracted responses, especially such innocuous-sounding ones as the recent *The New Schelling* (eds. Judith Norman and Alistair Welchman, Continuum, London and New York, 2004) and *Schelling Now* (ed. Jason M. Wirth, Indiana University Press, Bloomington and Indianapolis, 2005). Both books collect essays on Schelling's thought. *The New Schelling* presents essays principally though not exclusively drawn from European scholars. There are other signs of current interest in Schelling. Jason Wirth has written a Schelling book entitled *The Conspiracy of Life* (SUNY, Albany, 2003), and Elibron Books has just rereleased a late-nineteenth-century work of Eduard von Hartmann entitled *Schelling's Philosophisches System* (Boston, 2005). For Schelling studies, this represents a hurricane of activity. In comparison with Kant and Plato, the two principal thinkers I considered in connection with Schelling, two books of essays and a few books released in two years would signal a desert.

In the endnotes, I have discussed the work of Schelling scholars whose comments on the *Freedom Essay* merit thoughtful response. Happily, this includes virtually all such interpreters. One does not read Schelling without becoming captivated, and his thought requires unusual focus and discipline. In his last published work, the *Freedom Essay*, he draws upon so many sources and his arguments and accounts take so many twists that only the most careful attention can puzzle out his meaning. This concentration is rewarded with a concealed rigor of thought and expansiveness of imagination that is attained rarely if at all in other philosophers.

Yet this very idiosyncratic quality will, in my opinion, continue to keep Schelling out of the mainstream of philosophical thought, despite Heidegger's correct judgment that Schelling is the most creative, deepest, and farthest-reaching thinker of the age of German Idealism. Given the sameness of the central concepts, one can trace the development of German Idealism from Kant through Fichte to Hegel rather easily. All insisted upon systematic completeness, though only Hegel provided a system that could be called complete without equivocation. Kant and Fichte found systematic unity within the limits of rationality.

But even in Schelling's Fichtean period, there were unmistakable signs that his oddity would make him out of place both with Kant and Fichte, on one side, and with Hegel on the other. Fichte's *Anstoss* (check, resistance) may be likened to Kant's *Ding an sich* (thing in itself) since both limit the range of rationality from outside it. But neither can be assimilated to Schelling's irreducible remainders, such as the dark principle that the human being can never master, or indifference that lies on the nether side of both principles. Nor can Schelling's system be assimilated to Hegel's. For Schelling, artistic expression is co-primordial with philosophical expression, while for Hegel artistic expression is a stage (a very high one, but a stage nevertheless) on the way to spirit as self-conscious reason's self-completion. The truth about Schelling is that his thought is always out of place, in Greek *atopon*—strange, literally "out of place" or even "having no place."

His thought is, however, required from time to time, when another kind of strangeness pervades. More particularly, I suggest that Schelling's thought is required when the philosophical landscape seems most eviscerated. As I write this, most major movements seem eviscerated, seem to be playing themselves out, however thoughtfully. A return to Schelling at such times provides a source of rejuvenation. In Schelling, a rapture that is genuinely philosophical underlies and inspires philosophical inquiry. I cannot imagine that Schelling has found many readers in the Anglo-American philosophical orientation. The kind of training provided in this latter tradition (I was exposed to such training) is no more suitable for the exegesis of texts from the history of philosophy as the former, Continental training is for understanding whatever nicer points one finds in the journal *Philosophy*. Cambridge University Press, which has issued volumes of essays on many major figures from philosophy's history (virtually all of these collections are regrettable in my view), has not seen fit to release one on Schelling. I am thankful.

Nevertheless, the earliest impulses found in the Anglo-American orientation are quite impassioned and muscular. The task was to purge philosophy of metaphysics and to establish philosophy on a sound logical and scientific basis. With the vigor of Hume consigning books of divinity or school metaphysics to the flames at the conclusion of his 1748 *Inquiry* (though without any of Hume's subtlety, insight or playfulness), the logical positivists and their followers devised principles of various kinds in order to redirect philosophy. The successors of Carnap, et al, have done their share of interesting work (Quine, Davidson, Sellars). As painful as it was to read their work, I always felt that I was in touch with a living, committed force. However, I discern little of that initial life now. I have heard of no books or papers of late that I simply must read in order to become aware of that philosophical impulse.

Since texts from the history of philosophy comprise an essential component of our own philosophizing for those of us whose orientation is Continental, we are less likely to engage in two practices of our Anglo-American counterparts. We are less likely to dismiss a text based upon its age. We are also less likely to look for "positions" or "theses," seeking rather to interpret the texts for various kinds of insight they offer. We are more concerned with the way philosophy's past remains alive in us than we are with how methodological advances have rendered this past obsolete. Nevertheless, though I am much more sympathetic to our position, I too sense a certain disorientation. However, on our side we have begun to turn back to Schelling. This is a sign of recognition and health, and the results have been both happy and promising.

Heidegger's challenge to Western metaphysics issued from at least as deep a passion, though from a very different standpoint, as that of Carnap, who mangled Heidegger's work so crudely and so unjustly that one wonders whether a bad conscience was concealed beneath it.[1] For Heidegger, metaphysics could never be measured by formal logic, which he at one point called "an abortion of an abortion."[2] However, by virtue of its forgetfulness of the question of Being and concentrating instead upon beings, metaphysics as science of being exhausted itself in the early nineteenth century. It did so first in the Hegelian system where it was brought to completeness, and took its last gasp as "will to power" in Nietzsche's philosophy of the will. The richness of Heideggerian thought provided seeds for further development, both before and after the *Kehre* (turn). *Die Kehre* turned away from philosophy as thought of Being to thought as nearing its essence alongside but on separate mountain peaks from the essence of poetry.

Heidegger's destruction (*Destruktion*) of the history of philosophy in *Sein und Zeit* and beyond did not resemble that of Carnap and the verificationists in the least. Instead, it sought to investigate many of the West's major thinkers in order to detect the necessary forgetfulness of Being that allowed for metaphysics in the first place, and to recover those resources for thought that either remained or could be excavated from their thought. This involved such daring exegeses as *Kant and the Problem of Metaphysics* in which transcendental imagination is declared to be the "unknown root" of sensibility and understanding (a conclusion from which Kant "recoiled"), and such daring translations of the Greek, especially in the so-called (and wrongly called) Presocratic Greeks, as "Man dwells in the nearness of god" for "*ethos anthropo daimon*"[3] instead of the usual bromide, "a man's character is his fate."

Here I must reveal a most embarrrasing episode. I was a graduate student at Duquesne University in the early 1970s. Many of us were captivated by Heidegger, many by Husserl. Most of us came to love both. One afternoon, during a discussion in the Student Union dining area, one of our more passionate colleagues bounded to the table, slammed down a thick book, and announced portentously: "You are looking at the next big movement in Continental Philosophy." My turn came for a quick look. Even from the most cursory inspection, it was clear to me that the book was going nowhere. I replied something along the lines of the following: "Sorry to burst your bubble, but this one is dead in the water. It has absolutely no chance of any influence, and you can bet your own life and the lives of your loved ones on that."

The book's title was *Grammatology*, its author Jacques Derrida. So much for my confident, uncanny prescience. Derrida's influence pervaded Continental philosophy as practiced in America. Heidegger's *Destruktion* became "deconstruction."

Here is not the place to offer either a defense or a critique. Since deconstruction is an event that remains alive in so many regions of thought, I am not at all sure that such comments would matter in any case (though I opine that its decidedly mixed effect has been less than salutary on the whole). Unlike Heidegger's *Destruktion* (or destruction), "deconstruction" consisted and consists of exposing the often unacknowledged presuppositions that activate any discourse, but which cannot be accounted for within that discourse. The term caught the popular *Zeitgeist*, and can be read in newspapers, heard on talk shows, and seen in advertisements. It has become synonymous with "criticize," and is frequently used to impress the less learned.

On the other hand, by providing a powerful critical tool, the deconstruction of the dominant discourses of Western metaphysics allowed for the entrance of previously marginalized and suppressed voices into the philosophical arena (e.g., feminist, African-American, post-colonialist, queer). While there is no question of the life-force of this entry and of the ongoing need for continued philosophical openness, I do not sense the initial urgency. Those once-marginalized voices now speak at the table. Many if not most of these vocalize the latent and/or express oppressiveness inherent in the history of Western metaphysics to which their forbears fell victim.

Metaphysics—meaning the way of thought dominating the modern history of philosophy from Descartes through German Idealism—is simply no longer practiced, either by Anglo-American or Continental practitioners of philosophy. It may be studied, it may be criticized, it may be mined for arguments and new insights, but no one is going to write anything like a *Critique of Pure Reason*, or for that matter an *Inquiry Concerning Human Understanding*. In both of the aforementioned works, human reason reaches its limit and so must admit its ignorance on fundamental matters. Both works are profoundly Socratic in that sense. Hume's *Inquiry* provides a litany of statements asserting our thoroughgoing ignorance of matters of importance, including our self-knowledge.[4] As is well known, Kant's first *Critique* also declares our self-ignorance, and insists upon our ignorance of the Ideas of the soul, the world and God (the objects of special metaphysics) as well. Seeing them together, one can see a foreshadowing of the end of metaphysics from within metaphysics in their work.

Metaphysics has presaged its own end in the work of its greatest practitioners. Metaphysics has been declared to be at an end by philosophers in both strains of contemporary Western philosophy. Thus, its major discourses have putatively been "undermined" in many ways. However, the once-vaunted energy behind its replacement seems to have lost much of its power. I will leave aside Anglo-American thought, for which traditional metaphysics holds little if any living interest. The influence of deconstruction upon Continental philosophy in America has often treated the texts of the traditional Western philosophical canon as corpses for dissection, though Derrida insisted—especially toward the end of his life—that this was never his intention. In any case, this frequent disrespect regarding our metaphysical tradition pervades Continental philosophy today and calls for a response. Schelling's thought stands at the crossroads. It incorporates the history of metaphysics as it draws upon non- and extra-metaphysical sources, bringing them together with his own unique vision. As an undeconstructable rejuvenator, his untimely work has become timely.

Heidegger's 1937 Schelling book planted a key seed for much of this renewed interest. His interpretation presented his *Destruktion* at its pinnacle, revealing heretofore unsuspected resources in Schelling. Every criticism one might make of his conclusions, particularly concerning his negative assessment of the final two sections of the *Freedom Essay*, are possible only as a result of the clarity, the rigor, and the daring of his reading. The same comment holds in virtually every case, even and especially in his Plato interpretations, which are his weakest in my opinion. It seems to me that at least two books by John Sallis provide models for the reincorporation of Schelling, especially the *Freedom Essay*, into post-Heideggerian philosophical thought.

The first, entitled *Delimitations: Phenomenology and the End of Metaphysics* (Bloomington, 1995), concludes with a chapter on the *Freedom Essay*. It does so precisely because Schelling's thought, while remaining within German Idealism's metaphysical trajectory in certain ways, cannot be contained within it. Sallis points especially to the role of divine imagination. As we have seen repeatedly, God as existing (light) requires a ground different from himself (darkness) in order to give birth to himself and, with this birth of himself, the entire order of creation comes forth as well. Sallis writes:

> Now the way of divine imagination has been drawn: the procession of things from the divine imagination is no mere production, analogous, for instance, to the way human phantasy produces its figments of the mind.

> On the contrary, everything—both God and the world, is referred back to the ground, and the imagination that is the other side, as it were, of this reference can only draw from the ground, from its secluded depths, what it casts as image in nature. . . .[5]

The secluded ground serves as both life-giving source and as irreducible remainder, escaping determination even as it makes determination possible. That is, the dark ground escapes metaphysics. It is *other* than being.

While Sallis does not interpret Schelling's "indifference" quite as negatively as Heidegger does, he wonders whether indifference amounts to "Summoning up the spectre of metaphysics at the limit of metaphysics."[6] He concludes his book by wondering whether, instead of positing the prior non-antithetical unity of indifference, Schelling's

> hovering (*schweben*) . . . between the self-secluding ground and the image-charged reflection . . . would be capable of stationing itself at the limit that Schelling's thought marks so forcefully?[7]

I certainly find the recourse to image-making as crucial to the overcoming of metaphysical thought. Also, I find the conclusion *as a living question* to be essential to our task of thinking today. However, I would ask: Is the spectre that indifference might summon very frightening?

Chorology (Bloomington, 1999) is a reinterpretation of Plato's *Timaeus* (Sallis calls it a "reinscription" of Schelling) that concludes by bringing Schelling's thought to bear upon his and our own attempt to think the *khora*. After demonstrating the many ways Schelling wrestled with the thought of the *khora* from the beginning of his philosophical career, even before his first publication, Sallis' four "preconclusions" concern (1) Schelling's avoidance of an ontic interpretation of the Platonic *eide*; (2) his awareness of the "pre-cosmic, pre-genetic" dimension opened up by the discourses around the chorology; (3) his peculiar way of referring to the third kind in the language of substance and matter; and (4) most significantly, Schelling's "scant attention to the artistry and poetry of the *Timaeus*,"[8] which is astonishing since Schelling is the philosopher with the greatest esteem and feeling for the aesthetic.

What I would call *Chorology*'s conclusion proper is introduced by the following two questions, again essential for our philosophizing today:

> But what about the beyond of the Schellingian reinscription, this powerful appropriation that to an unprecedented degree lets what was called

> *khora* come again to a manifestness befitting its seclusion? What about this beyond of this reinscription that ventured to reconstitute something like the chorology in the midst—indeed at the very center—of modern thought and that seriously faltered perhaps only in not shaping its discourse to the retreat of the *khora*, that is in not openly declaring itself a bastardly discourse?[9]

Sallis' seminal *Being and Logos: Reading the Platonic Dialogues* (Bloomington, 1996) addresses itself particularly to the "artistry and poetry" of the Platonic dialogues, which he regards as equal in philosophical importance to the *logoi*. This way of approaching Plato is *ours*, belonging specifically to *our* age, and still retains its initial force. The reinscription of Schelling by Sallis at the conclusion of his *Timaeus* interpretation is, for us, a recovery of a pre-archaic *arkhe* in a *logos* that repels *logos*. In more contemporary terms, it is an exemplary showing and enactment of language at the limit. I can only wonder whether the "bastardly discourse" (*logismo notho*) is already written into the *Freedom Essay* by virtue of the very matter it treats. Perhaps it is one of the "many things that could have been expressly saved from misinterpretation" (410n) that had to await its time.

Our age has granted the opportunity for an appropriate return to Schelling now, reading him in new ways.

Notes

INTRODUCTION

1. *Philosophische Untersuchungen über das Wesen der menschlichen Freiheit und die damit zusammenhängenden Gegenstände* (1809). (*Philosophical Investigations concerning the Essence of Human Freedom and the Objects connected with it*), which I will continue to call by the much more manageable *Freedom Essay.*

2. There is one central feature (or absence of a feature) that I have consciously retained: no comparisons with Hegel can be found in this reading. I urge the reader not to assume the slightest disrespect for that great thinker, from whom I have learned so much. Rather, in my view Schelling must be taken on his own terms, not as a mere steppingstone toward his contemporary whose external influence is far greater. In this, I stand with many contemporary Schelling readers, as is clear in the endnotes and conclusion.

3. Martin Wallen, "The Electromagnetic Orgasm and the Narrative of Primordiality," in *Schelling Now: Contemporary Readings*, ed. Jason Wirth (Bloomington: Indiana University Press, 2005), 130. Wallen also observes that the "fragmentary and provisional nature" characterizes virtually all of Schelling's works (131).

4. Martin Heidegger, *Schellings Abhandlung Über das Wesen der menschlichen Freiheit* (Tübingen, 1971), 4. (My translation)

I. THE UNFOLDING OF THE TASK

1. All page references to Schelling's *Freedom Essay* are to Friedrich Wilhelm Joseph von Schelling, *Schellings Werke*, ed. Manfred Schröter (München: E. H. Beck, 1959), IV, VII. All other references to Schelling are from the same edition.

2. Schelling makes few express references to Heraclitus. However, I shall declare their kinship with some confidence. While the express textual evidence is thin, I cannot help but suppose that Heraclitean fragments silently but clearly animate several of Schellingian focal points.

3. Schelling, I, I, 90.

4. In *Schelling and the End of Idealism* (Albany: SUNY, 1996), Dale E. Snow provides a sympathetic but critical commentary on Schelling's philosophical career, however much one might disagree with her on certain matters. Her study concludes with the insight, among others, that it is characterized by a gradual decline in his faith in reason that is strongest in his early work. His abiding willingness to attend to darkness, against which the possibility of system had to be given up, left him with a Christian metaphysics as a kind of default position: ". . . Schelling, like Fichte and other post-Kantians of the early nineteenth century, initially sees his vocation as not only the completion of Kant's philosophy but as constructing a philosophical system. And like Fichte, Schelling at the same time explores the concept of system itself. Yet it is not a defeat that Schelling never arrives at a system. Rather he eventually brings into question the possibility of systematic philosophy itself." She then quotes Joseph Esposito, who claimed that Schelling "probably" took German Idealism as far as it could go (2–3).

I find this aspect of her view "accurate" without being "true." System is not something "constructed" in Schelling, but rather—if indeed this expression serves—"discovered" and "articulated."

5. Schelling, III, V, 237.

6. Both "*O b j e k t*" and "*G e g e n s t a n d*" are presented as so spaced in the original.

7. Schelling, II, III, 364.

8. Ibid., 370.

9. This threefold suggests the three regions treated by the Kantian critiques: feeling in the *Critique of Judgment*, fact in the *Critique of Practical Reason*, and concept in the *Critique of Pure Reason*.

10. Schelling, III, V, 215.

11. Immanuel Kant, *Critique of Pure Reason*, trans. Norman Kemp Smith (New York: St. Martin's Press, 1929), A401–2, emphasis in original.

12. Ibid., B421.

13. Rüdiger Bubner, ed. "Das älteste Systemprogramm," in *Hegel-Studien*, Beiheft 9 (Bonn, 1973), 264.

14. Ibid., 264–65.

15. Schelling, III, V, 384.

16. Ibid., 385.

17. Ibid., 405.

18. Schelling, II, III, 630.

19. See §59 of Kant's *Critique of Judgment.*

20. Schelling's citation read as follows: Sext. Empir. Adv. Grammatikos, L. I. c. 13, p. 238 ed. Fabric (337n).

21. "Regarding the formation (*Bildung*) of the elementary basic material of energy, if one wishes to draw a comparison with ancient philosophy in general one can equate (*gleichsetzen*) it earliest of all with the basic material of fire in the philosophy of Heraclitus." Werner Heisenberg, "Grundlegende Voraussetzungen in der Physik der Elementarteilchen," in *Martin Heidegger zum siebzigsten Geburtstag: Festschrift*, ed. Günther Neske (Pfullingen, 1959), 292.

22. An excellent example is W.V.O. Quine's influential "Two Dogmas of Empiricism," in which he writes, "I do, qua lay physicist, believe in physical objects and not in Homer's gods; and I consider it a scientific error to believe otherwise. But in point of epistemological footing the physical objects and the gods differ only in degree but not in kind. The *myth* of physical objects is epistemologically superior to most in that it has proved more efficacious than other myths as a device for working a manageable structure into the flux of experience" (*Philosophical Review* 60, 1951).

23. In the Third Antinomy, Kant takes special care *not* to assert either the reality of freedom or even its possibility: "What we have alone been able to show, and what we have alone been concerned to show, is that this antinomy rests on a sheer illusion, and that causality through freedom is at least *not incompatible with* nature" (Kant, *Critique of Pure Reason*, op. cit., A558, B586).

24. In *Republic* VI on the divided line, mathematical objects are located in the intelligible region but rank below the *eide* (forms). For Kant, mathematical concepts are pure (and exhibited in intuition) but are ruled by the pure concepts of the understanding.

25. In a recent and fascinating republication of Eduard von Hartmann's 1897 *Schelling's Philosophisches System* (Boston: Elibron Classics, 2005), the author concludes that Schelling's system fails because of a number of internal contradictions. (I cannot resist noting the irony of this criticism from a thinker whose work was dedicated to synthesizing Schopenhauer and Hegel.) "*Alle Versuche, die Schellingsche Geistesphilosophie der zweiten Periode zu verwerten und fortzubilden, sind bisher mit Recht gescheitert; die rechte Flügel der Schellingsche Schule, der sich auf Schelling's Bemuhumgen um die Restauration der gennanten Ideentrias stützt, ist unweigerlich durch die diesen innewohnende Widersprüche zur philosophichen Unfruchtbarkeit und Bedeutungslosigkeit verurteilt*" (221). ["All attempts to use and to build upon Schelling's philosophy of spirit of the second period have justly shattered; the

correct sail that supports Schelling's efforts in order to restore the idea-triad are undeniably condemned to philosophical unfruitfulness and insignificance due to indwelling contradictions."] While Hartmann pays more attention to other works of Schelling, his general condemnation certainly extends to the *Freedom Essay*. He does not see indwelling contradiction as a source of provocation, as I do here.

26. Aeschylus, *Agamemnon*, eds. J. D. Denniston and D. L. Page (Oxford: Clarendon Press, 1968), 31 (l. 177). Spacing of letters is in original.

II. FREEDOM, PANTHEISM, AND IDEALISM

1. The twentieth-century play by George Bernard Shaw bearing the name *Pygmalion* and the later play/film *My Fair Lady* was loosely based on the myth (*very* loosely based). As they may influence the reading of this name, it is worth noting that Schelling's reference is to Ovid's *Metamorphoses*, 10, 243ff, where the king carves an ivory statue of his ideal woman, who is then brought to life by Aphrodite. See *Oxford Classical Dictionary*, ed. S. Hornblower and A. Spawforth (Oxford: Oxford University Press, 2003), 1281.

2. Immanuel Kant, *Critique of Practical Reason*, trans. Lewis White Beck (New York: St. Martin's Press, 1956), 86.

3. In Kirk, G. S., Raven, J. E., and Schofield, M., eds., *The Presocratic Philosophers* (Cambridge: Cambridge University Press, 1983), 187.

4. "But if I investigate more precisely the relation of given cognitions (*Erkenntnisse*) in any judgment, and distinguish it, as belonging to the understanding, from the relation belonging to the laws of reproductive imagination, which has only subjective validity, I find that a judgment is nothing but the manner in which given cognitions are brought to the objective unity of apperception. This is what is intended by the little-relational-word (*Verhältniswörtchen*) 'is'" (Kant, *Critique of Pure Reason*, op. cit., B141–42).

5. Gottfried Leibniz, "Monadology," in *Eighteenth Century Philosophy*, ed. Lewis White Beck (New York: Free Press, 1966), 198.

6. These "meanings" are all present in modern philosophy. Soon, Schelling will recover a more original "meaning" as well: *muthos*.

7. In his *Schelling: An Introduction to the System of Freedom* (New Haven: Yale University Press, 1983), Alan White wrestles with the difficulty of Schellingian logic. This wrestling has its source, according to my view, in that he does not come to see Heraclitus as the source of Schelling's "ancient logic." Of course the often oracular Schelling never says so himself. However, after providing a critique of his general view of logic together with his examples, he also gives a more sympathetic interpretation, claiming "the possibility that Schelling intentionally presents inadequate logical arguments, perhaps in order to indicate . . . that such reasoning is

too closely related to the merely mechanical." While my interpretation rejects the notion of the inadequacy of these arguments in light of the Heraclitean reflection, White is certainly correct in noting its directing thought decisively away from any mechanical interpretation. His work also deserves praise for reading the *Freedom Essay* dialogically.

8. Perhaps in the *Critique of Practical Reason*, in which the *synthetic* moral law renders the thought of an immoral deed self-contradictory, the two are indeed one.

9. Schelling, III, V, 324.

10. Kirk, Raven, and Schofield, *The Presocratic Philosophers*, 188.

11. Ibid., p. 187.

III. THE ACCOUNT OF THE POSSIBILITY OF EVIL

1. Schelling, I, II, 66.

2. F. W. J. Schelling, *Philosophical Investigations into the Nature of Human Freedom*, trans. J. Gutmann (Chicago: Open Court, 1936), 357n (Schelling pagination).

3. Schelling notes further ways in which his prior systematic writings both differ from but also supplement Fichte's. Fichte's idealism presented its "subjective" side, while Schelling's earlier *Ideen zu einer Philosophie der Natur* (1797) provided its objective side (Schelling, III, IV, 5).

4. Ibid., 114.

5. Ibid., 146–47.

6. Spacing of "*s e i e n d*" in original.

7. Schelling, III, IV, 163.

8. Ibid., 203–4.

9. G. W. F. Hegel, *Vorlesungen über die Geschichte der Philosophie*, Band III (Leipzig, 1971), 619. The entire quote reads: "Schelling has made known an individual (*einzelne*) essay concerning freedom, which is of a profound and speculative kind; it stands, however, for itself on its own. Philosophy can develop nothing individual." In his 1936 Schelling book, Heidegger will argue the opposite, namely ". . . the truth is that there was seldom a thinker who fought so passionately ever since his earliest period for his one and unique standpoint." See Martin Heidegger, *Schelling's Treatise on the Essence of Human Freedom*, trans. Joan Stambaugh (Athens, OH: Ohio University Press, 1985), 6.

10. Schelling, III, V, 274.

11. See chapter 6 of my *Imagination and Depth in Kant's Critique of Pure Reason* (New York: Peter Lang, 1994).

12. Kant, *Critique of Pure Reason*, op. cit., A150.

13. Schelling, I, I, 366–67.

14. Ibid., 367.

15. That Schelling was intrigued and provoked by Plato's *Timaeus* is clear from the relatively recent discovery and publication of his early Plato studies. See F. W. J. Schelling, "*Timaeus*," ed. Hartmut Buchner (Stuttgart-Bad Cannstatt: Frommann-Holzboog, 1994). An excellent and thorough account of this role can be found in the final chapter of John Sallis' *Chorology: On Beginning in Plato's Timaeus* (Bloomington: Indiana University Press, 1999), especially 154–67. Sallis shows how Schelling's deep interest in this dialogue was present in his work "from the beginning, from before the beginning . . ." (156).

16. Kant, *Critique of Practical Reason*, op. cit., 91.

17. The first discourse presents the form of the eternal intelligible paradigm (*nous*), and the visible cosmos is seen through *aisthesis*. These ways of access, however, cannot be available for beholding the realm of the necessary, called by many names: the third form, the *khora*, the receptacle (*hupodokhe*) of all becoming, its wetnurse. Without this realm, the original two forms could have done no forming. The receptacle has no instances of itself. By means of it, nothing whatsoever can be seen. Yet it always receives all things, and never in any way takes on any characteristic similar to any of the things that enter it (50b9–c2). It is a form that does no forming and provides no way of seeing at all. However, in its radical neutrality it does allow things, after a fashion, to be seen from themselves. By contrast with the clarity of the earlier forms, Timaeus calls this third form difficult (*khalepos*) and obscure (*amudros*).

18. Schelling claims that "all philosophers say this" about God, which might make Hume, for example, stir from his eternal rest.

19. This is a creative appropriation of the Leibnizian monad.

20. In his superb chapter on the *Freedom Essay*, Werner Marx places special emphasis on what he calls "divine freedom": "I am convinced that God's inexplicable and sudden emergence as eternal oneness is intricately connected with that meaning of his essence, which is, for Schelling, the realization of a special kind of freedom. Indeed it is the lightninglike emergence that characterizes that aspect of freedom which the tradition denotes with the concept of 'spontaneity.' The emphasis here is not so much on a 'beginning' but rather on a 'being able to begin.' Why is it possible that there *can be* a beginning at all? Schelling's answer to that question, which still accords the mystery its due, might perhaps be that a beginning can be made because divine freedom emerges in the leap from God as the nonground (*Ungrund*) to God as the 'eternal oneness.'" See *The Philosophy of F. W. J. Schelling*, trans. Thomas Nenon (Bloomington: Indiana University Press, 1984), 68.

What I find especially striking about Marx's reading is that he does not take up the mythical nature of Schelling's speech thematically (except in passing on 47), but his interpretation is remarkably attuned to this language and to this way of philosophizing.

21. Schelling, IV, VII, 184n.

22. Here Schelling seems to mean something other than *khora* when he writes of Plato's "matter" (*Materie*). Rather, in this context "matter" refers to the element-traces "before" having been given form. Like *khora* however, Schelling dwells within the horizon of—perhaps the horizonless—errant cause.

23. John, 3:16.

24. Wirth's noteworthy interpretation of Schelling's treatment of language exemplifies the resources in Schelling for contemporary thought. He shows how Schellingian language, thoughtfully considered, opens out into the realm of art by its very nature. Vowel, in German, is *Selbstlauter*—self-sound. Consonant is *Mitlauter*—with-sound. He writes:

> Humans can break the unity of the Word and thereby just speak their own words and flee to the periphery . . . and dwell in the perverse house of vowels. . . . But poets . . . can hear and articulate the consonant of darkness as it expresses itself in the vowel of light.

Darkness is the basis independent of light. In language, nature is comprised of inarticulate consonants. It is nature before nature, that is, before nature comes to light. The human being, in particular the poet, attends to the darkness that exists separately from his existence, that is, to the inarticulate nature in him. In speaking the real Word, the poet brings forth nature in its originary sense as art. See Jason M. Wirth, "Animalization: Schelling and the Problem of Expressivity," in *Schelling Now*, ed. Jason Wirth, op. cit., p. 88.

25. John, 3:16.

26. This is one of the very few places where I find myself in puzzled but also in firm disagreement with Wirth. Throughout "Animalization: Schelling and the Problem of Expressivity" (*Schelling Now*, ed. Jason Wirth [Bloomington, 2005]), Wirth identifies the force of dark with "the Good" and light with "the True." I could not find any textual support for these identifications in the *Freedom Essay* or elsewhere. Goodness emerges from the subordination by the principle of light of the dark principle, which always remains. Evil consigns the principle of light to the periphery, elevating selfhood over light and the universal will.

More puzzling yet is Wirth's explanatory endnote, which reads: "I am using the Good and the True in the manner specific to German idealism and hence roughly in accord with Kant's deployment of the terms" (96). Fichte is usually regarded as German idealism's first expositor. Further, Kant deploys "the Good" and "the True" rarely if ever, speaking rather of moral goodness and theoretical truth. If we were to read these "capitalized" terms into Kant, "the Good" is always deployed morally, just as "the True" is always regarded theoretically.

27. After noting that the metaphorics of birth do not merely constitute "rhetorical disguise for philosophical concepts, but rather correspond to a 'demetaphysization' ('*Entmetaphyaizierung*') of the problem of individuation," Francesco Moiso observes: "In the place of imagination (*Einbildung*) as the 'stamp' of the essence upon the form, *Ein-bildung* lets the One emerge from its concealment in the ground." See Francesco Moiso, "Geometrische Notwendigkeit, Naturgesetz und Wirklichkeit. Ein Weg zur Freiheitsschrift," in *Schellings Weg zur Freiheitsschrift: Legende und Wirklichkeit*, ed. Hans Michael Baumgartner and Wilhelm G. Jacobs (Stuttgart-Bad Cannstatt: Frommann-Holzboog, 1996), 182.

28. A Kantian reference is germane: the human being can subordinate the moral law, which holds universally, to the satisfaction of pathological desires, which is in every case particular.

IV. THE ACCOUNT OF THE ACTUALITY OF FREEDOM

1. Schelling, I, I, 242n.

2. Immanuel Kant, *Critique of Judgment*, trans. by J. H. Bernard (New York, 1951), 249–50.

3. In the myth of Er, Odysseus has the final choice. Purified of love of honor in his previous life, he seeks carefully and finds the soul of a private man who minds his own business. This soul was neglected by the others, and he chose it happily, saying that he would have chosen it had he been first (Plato, *Republic* 620c2–d2).

4. Schelling's Christian references attract certain theologians and can repel philosophers. What is at stake, however, in the work of Schelling is *philosophy*, the articulation of the whole as living whole; in the *Freedom Essay*, the image of "the exemplary and divine man" must be understood as belonging to philosophy. Indeed, the way in which this image is seen as an image provides a shining opportunity to illustrate the meeting of Greek and modern with respect to proximity with the divine.

5. Judith Norman supplies a particularly acute interpretation of temporality in Schelling: ". . . [God] tucks a past under his present in order that he can exist. Schelling calls this negative force a 'repression' into the base of God's existence."

This is an odd conception of the past: the past is not just the chronological but the transcendental ground of the present, the condition of its possibility. This means that the past is not a past present, it never was a "now." Rather, it is always already past; it is a unique dimension separated from the present by ontological difference. We experience the present as an outward expansion, driving us forward;

but, Schelling argues, we also feel the heaviness of this past as a permanent heaviness or undertow, a constant but subliminal sense of the melancholy that infuses all things. "Schelling and Nietzsche: Willing and Time," in *The New Schelling*, eds. J. Norman and A. Welchman (London: Continuum Publishers, 2004), 97.

6. For a discussion of this, Schelling's somewhat odd translation of *khora*, see the observations toward the beginning of chapter 6.

7. In "'Philosophy Become Genetic,': The Physics of the World Soul," Iain Hamilton Grant not only engages this point expertly but locates an apposite Platonic reference: ". . . the conflict of the forces cannot be assumed to be such as to maintain indefinitely the current relations amongst the series of organizations on the earth, and will give rise, come the *Philosophical Inquiries*, to world-disorder, such as occurs when the World Soul loses control in the *Statesman*." (In *The New Schelling*, op. cit., p. 143.)

8. In "Schelling's Metaphysics of Evil," Joseph P. Lawrence contrasts Schelling's conception of evil from that of Kant, who properly situated evil in the rational sphere but "lets the actual content of evil collapse once again into the sphere of animal desire." He writes, "In Schelling's treatise on human freedom, a prolonged discussion of the metaphysical possibility of evil, that is, an exploration of the temptations that stood before God himself, precedes any discussion of radical evil (VII, 357–73). The self-constitution of evil is a mediated one. Eternity itself presupposes the abyss of an eternal past. What surfaces in man, and constitutes the real possibility of evil, is the oldest and most hidden part of the ground, that principle of radical freedom which, preceding all causality, is capable of lacerating the world" (183). See "Schelling's Metaphysics of Evil," in *The New Schelling*, op. cit., 182–83.

While I endorse and praise Lawrence's notion of a freedom that is ontologically prior to moral freedom, and his striking Schellingian imagery of world laceration, I must wonder about his claim that the principle of radical freedom is situated "in the oldest and most hidden part of the ground." According to my reading, the ground is ontologically prior to all temporal determinations. Radical freedom, rather, cannot be located anywhere (that is why it is called radical), but extends itself out of the abyssal difference of existence and ground. They are both in God, but are divided in the human being.

V. THE REAL CONCEPT OF FREEDOM—THE FORMAL SIDE

1. Dale E. Snow notes, "Here in *Of Human Freedom* being is supplanted by becoming, and concepts by metaphors. A living reality cries out for a living language to reflect it, and it is clearly difficult for Schelling—a failed poet in his youth—to rise to the demands of his subject" (Snow, *Schelling and the End of Ideal-*

ism, 178–79). These remarks occur in the context of her discussion of the reality of evil and Schelling's "images of perversion and inversion." She proceeds to claim that with these, Schelling was unable to address the origin of evil (a debatable claim), though she credits it with being superior to other theories of evil.

Once again, she deserves much praise, in my view, for noting the requirements of a language that would be faithful to its subject matter, and her criticisms of scholars who fail to note this are decisive. I would go much further: the language of the *Freedom Essay* is by nature mythical, and its "images" are not images of originals but images for which the originals are necessarily absent and/or concealed.

2. J. G. Fichte's "First, absolutely unconditioned fundamental principle," is "The I posits its own being absolutely." J. v. G. Fichte, *Grundlage der gesamten Wissenschaftslehre* (Hamburg: F. Meiner, 1970), 11, 18. As is well known, this first principle serves to regulate the second and third principles in their interdetermination, and to found practical philosophy, the law of which is independent of time. Here I only wish to point out the timelessness and unconditionality of the primal act of self-positing. Schelling's early work as a Fichtean embraced these thoughts, which he later appropriated creatively in the *Freedom Essay*.

3. This is perhaps the deepest interpretation of Kant's denial of theoretical knowledge of freedom, yet the need for asserting it in the practical realm. The character of this need, to be sure, is presented as practical, but if this practical need is understood as a way of bringing together reason and desire for the sake of the most well-lived life, then perhaps the practical need is at bottom aesthetical. There are certainly passages in the *Critique of Judgment* that bear this out, especially in Section Fifty-Nine. For if freedom could be accounted for by something antecedent to it, it would not be freedom.

VI. THE DESCRIPTION OF THE MANIFESTATION OF EVIL IN HUMANITY

1. St. Thomas Aquinas, *The Basic Writings of St. Thomas Aquinas*, ed. Anton Pegis (New York, 1945), 152.

2. Ibid., 166.

3. This is not even to mention the relation of prime matter to God, despite its attribution to God in *Treatise on Creation*.

4. "*V o r*" is spaced in the original.

5. In his thoughtfully genealogical essay titled "*Vom Ursprung des Bösen zum Wesen der menschlichen Freiheit oder Transzendentalphilosophie und Metaphysik*," Wilhelm G. Jacobs locates Schelling's concern with the role of sin in relation to freedom as early as 1792, in his dissertation (written in Latin), an interpretation

of the third book of Genesis. "[Schelling] does not use the word 'fall into sin' (*Sündenfall*); he also does not regard the story (*Erzählung*) as one of historical fact, but rather as a mythical story concerning the origin of human freedom." In *Schellings Weg zur Freiheitsschrift: Legende und Wirklichkeit*, ed. Hans Michael Baumgartner and Wilhelm G. Jacobs (Stuttgart-Bad Cannstatt: Frommann-Holzboog, 1996), 13.

6. "Know yourself, nothing in excess" shows itself first as seriousness, later as playfulness in Plato. For a wonderful combination of the two, see *Phaedrus* 230a, where Socrates explains his bond to the Delphic oracle as he dismisses those who are sophisticated (*sophismenoi*).

7. Xenophon, *Symposium*, trans. C. L. Brownson and O. J. Todd (New York, 1922), IV. 64–V8.

VII. GOD AS MORAL BEING—THE NATURE OF THE WHOLE WITH RESPECT TO FREEDOM

1. Heidegger, *Schellings Abhandlung Über das Wesen der menschlichen Freiheit*, op. cit., p. 191.

2. Ibid., 192.

3. Ibid., 130.

4. Ibid., 194.

5. Ibid., 194.

6. Wirth's reversal of the Schellingian "veil of melancholy spread out over the whole of nature" is particularly thought-provoking. Reading this melancholy back into the indifference out of which all things emerge and to which all return, Wirth finds a rebirth of *comedy* in the *Freedom Essay*:

> It is also the beginning of life becoming comedy as the heroic strivings of the understanding collapse back into the fundament of its origin. In comedy one no longer has the thematic selectivity that a system demands.

Wirth proceeds to implicitly interpret Schelling's derivative absoluteness of all creatures, his A/a, in this way: "each and every opaque monad—expresses the silent, *comic* heart of nature." He senses the beginning "of the comic nature of a positive philosophy, of nature's free and miraculous expressivity." He calls Schelling's system of freedom not just comic but "tragicomic," since all creatures crash against their limit. But even this crash belongs to nature's expressivity. See "Animalization: Schelling and the Problem of Expressivity," in *Schelling Now*, ed. Jason Wirth, op. cit., 92.

I find the comic Schelling most suggestive. Along with Sallis at the close of *Chorology*, I wonder why Schelling himself did not note this. After all, he concluded his University Studies with the following:

> Even though the public at large may find it hard to grasp that art is a necessary, integral part of a state founded on Ideas, we should at least recall the example of antiquity, when festivals, public monuments, dramatic performances, and other communal activities together made up a single, universal objective and living work of art (F. W. J. Schelling, *On University Studies*, trans. E. S. Morgan [Athens, OH, 1966]), 151.

Surely Schelling knew that the dramatic performances at the Dionysian festival consisted daily of three tragedies and a comedy. The forgetfulness of comedy in relation to philosophy is itself a matter that calls for thought. Although Aristophanes played a major role in the Hegelian system, Wirth's essay strongly suggests that comedy may lie more nearly at the heart of Schelling's work.

7. Unlike Snow's commentary, Andrew Bowie's is an ongoing engagement putting Schelling's thought into critical dialogue with both his contemporaries and with ours (on both sides of the divide), with frequent evaluation of what he sees as Schelling's strengths and shortcomings. For those of us who see Schelling not as primarily a historical figure of a bygone era, as Bowie often does, but as a contemporary, he certainly has something to offer. An example of one of his best insights, despite the unwarranted opening swipe at Schelling's philosophy of nature: "We are not going to arrive at a philosophy of nature that wholly overcomes the regression to pre-Kantianism; but Schelling makes more unsentimental sense of the need not to repress the nature of which we are an aspect than almost any other modern philosopher. Such philosophy is not merely literary, nor is it simply dependent on analogy: whilst it gains its power from its metaphorical resources, it also, at the same time and in the same texts, doggedly pursues answers to conceptual problems." Andrew Bowie, *Schelling and Modern European Philosophy* (New York, 1993), 190.

VIII. INDIFFERENCE AND THE BIRTH OF LOVE

1. Heidegger, *Schellings Abhandlung Über das Wesen der menschlichen Freiheit*, op. cit., 195.

2. Wirth writes, "The original judgment, *Gut* and *Schlecht*, the affirmation of difference and dismissal without prosecution of the identity mongers, is spoken from a great health, from the exuberance of the Good beyond good and evil. Its speaking is fundamentally affirmative, the holy 'yes-saying.' It speaks from the place that Schelling in the *Freedom* essay called 'the highest point of the whole investigation' (406), namely love" (*The Conspiracy of Life: Meditations on Schelling and His Time* [Albany, 2003], 179–80). The book could not be more aptly named:

"con-spire" has the doubled sense of breathing together and of a prior "plot" by which forces not of our making bring life forth. The genitive can also be read both ways, either as suggesting that life itself is a conspiracy, or that the aforementioned forces joined for the sake of life.

The chapter from which this citation is drawn (Chapter 6: Evil) is written primarily in terms of the image of sickness/health, and engages many other thinkers. In so doing, it provides a most worthy additional exegetical perspective to this one.

3. Marx writes, "Human freedom is further determined by its position in relation to nature [as it also is by its position in relation to the divine]. This position likewise can only be understood against the background of Schelling's eschatological conception as a whole" (Marx, op. cit., 79–80). In one of my few sharp disagreements with Marx's interpretation, I do not find what he calls an "eschatological conception of the whole" in the *Freedom Essay*, nor do I see how such a conception sheds light upon the *topos* of the human. Though Schelling has written of a *distant* future in which God is all in all, I interpret this as a mythical, vicarious image for human beings in *this life*. Final purpose is not, considered for itself, a beyond or a future, however distant. It pertains only to time-bound humanity. The regress to the original *Ungrund*, a "beginning before all beginning" speaks rather to an *archae*ology.

4. Kirk, Raven, and Schofield, op. cit., 192 (Fr. 207), translation mine.

5. Schelling, IV, VIII, 204.

6. Ibid., 201.

7. "*Dia-*" means "through" or "by means of." "*Nous*," often translated as "intellect," but should rather be thought as perception generally, since its verb form usually means "perception by the eye."

8. In "Reading Schelling after Heidegger," Peter Warnek brings the notion of conversation together with both the subject matter of the *Freedom Essay* and with the contemporary problematic of reading: "Reading can no longer be conceived of simply as hermeneutic retrieval (detective work); rather, it occurs more originally through an act of 'creative' appropriation in which the movement of the thinking is repeated. Reading must repeat (or translate) the work *freely*, which is to say that it must already venture beyond talking *about* philosophy and become the (re-) enactment of philosophy as freedom." See "Reading Schelling After Heidegger: The Freedom of Cryptic Dialogue," in *Schelling Now*, ed. Jason Wirth, op. cit., 170.

9. Schelling, IV, VIII, 203.

10. Similarly, it recalls the divine madness of the poets as discussed in the *Ion*. In their right mind, the poets are quite ordinary, but under the sway of divine madness, they have many useful things to convey to humankind. See especially Plato, *Ion* 533c9–535a2.

11. Admittedly, this is an unusual translation. However, it retains the various senses of *Bild*, the word around which the entire passage turns. A looser one, eas-

ier to follow but not as faithful to Schelling's careful choices, might read, "forming the understanding as it glances into the archetype."

12. Persephone returns to the sun every nine years to mete out punishments; their souls become those of great kings. Pindar, fragment 133.

13. This result, which I have presented algebraically, came from a diagram drawn on the earth. Socrates asks the boy to give the number of the side of a square with an area of 8. After the boy gives a plausible but incorrect answer (3), he admits his ignorance.

CONCLUSION

1. In this context, I vividly recall my 1965 Philosophy 101 class with the late Jerome Stolnitz, in one of the most compelling courses I have ever taken. Stolnitz would present one of the philosophers we were reading, then detail that author's strengths with such conviction that we were entirely persuaded of the author's wisdom. Then he would present a point-by-point demolition of those strengths, convincing us that the author was a fool. The next class would find him answering the objections one by one, again in a marvelous manner.

The only philosopher he did not resurrect was Carnap. After detailing Carnap's criticisms and ridicule of Heidegger in a most eloquent manner, he convinced us that with Heidegger (whoever he was) we were dealing with a foolish incompetent who was obviously unaware of the basics of grammar, much less the wisdom of the verification principle. But in place of his usual rebuttal, Stolnitz said that he disdained to offer one because of the venality and incompetence of Carnap's critique. Carnap ran sentences together from different parts of the work, and did not attempt to gather the meaning of Heidegger's thought at all. If an undergraduate handed him such a paper, Stolnitz said, he would give it an "F."

Stolnitz was far from being a Heideggerian and equally far from being a friendly and approachable man. He was a great teacher, and I thank him.

2. Martin Heidegger, "Heraklit," in *Gesamtausgabe*, vol. 55 (Frankfurt am Main, 1975), 112–13.

3. Both of these prove quite accurate and rigorous.

4. "The most perfect philosophy of the natural kind only staves off our ignorance a little longer, as perhaps the most perfect philosophy of the moral and metaphysical kind serves only to discover larger and larger portions of it. Thus, the observation of human blindness and weakness is the result of all philosophy, and meets us, at every turn, in spite of our efforts to elude or avoid it." In David Hume, *An Inquiry Concerning Human Understanding* (Indianapolis: Bobbs-Merrill, 1977), 46.

5. John Sallis, *Delimitations: Phenomenology and the End of Metaphysics* (Bloomington: Indiana University Press, 1995), 230.

6. Ibid., 232.

7. Ibid., 233.

8. Sallis, *Chorology: On Beginning in Plato's Timaeus*, op. cit., 166.

9. Ibid., 167.

Selected Bibliography

Aeschylus. *Agamemnon*. J. D. Denniston and D. L. Page, eds. Oxford: Clarendon Press, 1968.

Baumgartner, Hans Michael, and Wilhelm G. Jacobs, eds. *Schellings Weg zur Freiheitsschrift: Legende und Wirklichkeit*. Stuttgart-Bad Cannstatt: Frommann-Holzboog, 1996.

Bowie, Andrew. *Schelling and Modern European Philosophy; an Introduction*. London: Routledge, 1993.

Fichte, J. G. *Grundlage der gesamten Wissenschaftslehre, als Handschrift für seins Zuhörer*. Hamburg: F. Meiner, 1970.

Freydberg, Bernard. *Imagination and Depth in Kant's Critique of Pure Reason*. New York: Peter Lang, 1994.

Grant, Iain Hamilton. "Philosophy Become Genetic: The Physics of the World Soul." In *The New Schelling*. J. Norman and A. Welchman, eds. London and New York: Continuum Publishers, 2004.

Hartmann, Eduard von. *Schelling's Philosophisches System*. Boston: Elibron Classics, 2005.

Hegel, G. W. F. *Vorlesungen über die Geschichte der Philosophie*, Band III. Leipzig: Verlag Phillip Reclam, 1971.

Hegel-Tage and Rüdiger Bubner. "Das älteste Systemprogramm; Studien zur Frühgeschichte des deutschen Idealismus." In *Hegel-Studien*, Beiheft 9. Bonn: Bouvier, 1973.

Heidegger, Martin. *Gesamtausgabe*, vol. 55, "Heraklit: [Freiburger Vorlesung, Sommersem. 1943 u. Sommersem. 1944]." Frankfurt am Main: V. Klostermann, 1975.

———. *Kant und das Problem der Metaphysik*. Frankfurt am Main: V. Klostermann, 1965.

———. *Schellings Abhandlung Über das Wesen der menschlichen Freiheit*. Tübingen: M. Niemeyer Verlag, 1971.

———. *Schelling's Treatise on the Essence of Human Freedom*. Series in Continental Thought, 8. J. Stambaugh, trans. Athens, OH: Ohio University Press, 1985.

Heisenberg, Werner. "Grundlegende Voraussetzungen in der Physik der Elementarteilchen." In *Martin Heidegger zum siebzigsten Geburtstag; Festschrift*. G. Neske, ed. Pfullingen: 1959.

Hume, David. *An Inquiry Concerning Human Understanding: With a Supplement, An Abstract of a Treatise of Human Nature*. C. W. Hendel, ed. Indianapolis: Bobbs-Merrill, 1977.

Jacobs, Wilhelm G. "*Vom Ursprung des Bösen zum Wesen der menschlichen Freiheit oder Transzendentalphilosophie und Metaphysik*." In *Schellings Weg zur Freiheitsschrift: Legende und Wirklichkeit*. Hans Michael Baumgartner and Wilhelm G. Jacobs, eds. Stuttgart-Bad Cannstatt: Frommann-Holzboog, 1996.

Kant, Immanuel. *Critique of Judgment*. J. H. Bernard, trans. New York: Hafner Publishing Co., 1951.

———. *Critique of Practical Reason*. Lewis White Beck, trans. New York: Liberal Arts Press, 1956.

———. *Critique of Pure Reason*. Norman Kemp Smith, trans. New York: St. Martin's Press, 1929.

———. *Foundations of the Metaphysics of Morals*. Lewis White Beck, trans. Indianapolis and New York: Library of Liberal Arts, 1956.

Kirk, G. S., Raven, J. E., and Schofield, M., eds. *The Presocratic Philosophers*. Cambridge: Cambridge University Press, 1983.

Lawrence, Joseph P. "Schelling's Metaphysics of Evil." In *The New Schelling*. J. Norman and A. Welchman, eds. London: Continuum, 2004.

Leibniz, G. W. "Monadology." In *Eighteenth Century Philosophy*. L. W. Beck, ed. New York: Free Press, 1966.

Marx, Werner. *The Philosophy of F. W. J. Schelling: History, System, and Freedom*. Thomas Nenon, trans. Bloomington: Indiana University Press, 1984.

Moiso, Francesco. "Geometrische Notwendigkeit, Naturgesetz und Wirklichkeit. Ein Weg zur Freiheitsschrift." In *Schellings Weg zur Freiheitsschrift: Legende und Wirklichkeit*. Hans Michael Baumgartner and Wilhelm G. Jacobs, eds. Stuttgart-Bad Cannstatt: Frommann-Holzboog, 1996.

Norman, Judith. "Schelling and Nietzsche: Willing and Time." In *The New Schelling*. J. Norman and A. Welchman, eds. London and New York: Continuum Publishers, 2004.

Norman, Judith, and Alistair Welchman, eds. *The New Schelling*. London: Continuum Publishers, 2004.

Plato. *Complete Works*. John M. Cooper, ed. Indianapolis: Hackett Publishing Company, Inc., 1997.

———. *Platonis Opera*. Vol. I–III. Ioannes Burnet, ed. Oxford: Oxford Classical Texts, 1967, 1968.

"Pygmalion." *The Oxford Classical Dictionary*. S. Hornblower and A. Spawforth, eds. Oxford: Oxford University Press, 2003.

Quine, W. V. O. "The Two Dogmas of Empiricism." In *Philosophical Review* 60, 1951.

Sallis, John. *Being and Logos: Reading the Platonic Dialogues*. Bloomington: Indianapolis University Press, 1996.

———. *Chorology: On Beginning in Plato's Timaeus*. Bloomington: Indiana University Press, 1999.

———. *Delimitations: Phenomenology and the End of Metaphysics*. Bloomington: Indiana University Press, 1995.

Schelling, F. W. J. *On University Studies*. E. S. Morgan, trans. Athens OH: Ohio University Press, 1966.

———. *Philosophical Investigations into the Nature of Human Freedom*. J. Gutmann, trans. Chicago: Open Court, 1936.

———. *Schelling's Werke, nach der Originalausgabe in neuer Anordnung*. Vol. I–VI. Manfred Schröter, ed. München: E. H. Beck, 1959.

———. *Timaeus*. Hartmut Buchner, ed. Stuttgart-Bad Cannstatt: Frommann-Holzboog, 1994.

Snow, Dale E. *Schelling and the End of Idealism*. SUNY series in Hegelian studies. Albany: SUNY Press, 1996.

St. Thomas Aquinas. *The Basic Writings of St. Thomas Aquinas*. A. Pegis, ed. New York: Random House, 1945.

Wallen, Martin. "The Electromagnetic Orgasm and the Narrative of Primordiality in Schelling's 1815 Cosmic History." In *Schelling Now: Contemporary Readings*. Jason Wirth, ed. Bloomington: Indiana University Press, 2005.

Warnek, Peter. "Reading Schelling After Heidegger: The Freedom of Cryptic Dialogue." In *Schelling Now: Contemporary Readings*. Jason Wirth, ed. Bloomington: Indiana University Press, 2005.

White, Alan. *Schelling: An Introduction to the System of Freedom*. New Haven: Yale University Press, 1983.

Wirth, Jason M. "Animalization: Schelling and the Problem of Expressivity." In *Schelling Now: Contemporary Readings*. Jason Wirth, ed. Bloomington: Indiana University Press, 2005.

———. *The Conspiracy of Life: Meditations on Schelling and His Time*. Albany: SUNY Press, 2003.

———, ed. *Schelling Now: Contemporary Readings*. Bloomington: Indiana University Press, 2005.

Xenophon. *Anabasis Books IV–VII, Symposium and Apology*. C. L. Brownson and O. J. Todd, eds. New York: G. P. Putnam, 1922.

Index